Accrual Practices and Reform Experiences in OECD Countries

This work is published under the responsibility of the Secretary-General of the OECD. The opinions expressed and arguments employed herein do not necessarily reflect the official views of OECD member countries or IFAC.

This document and any map included herein are without prejudice to the status of or sovereignty over any territory, to the delimitation of international frontiers and boundaries and to the name of any territory, city or area.

Please cite this publication as:
OECD/IFAC (2017), *Accrual Practices and Reform Experiences in OECD Countries*, OECD Publishing, Paris.
http://dx.doi.org/10.1787/9789264270572-en

ISBN 978-92-64-27055-8 (print)
ISBN 978-92-64-27057-2 (PDF)

Co-edition with International Federation Accountants (IFAC)

The statistical data for Israel are supplied by and under the responsibility of the relevant Israeli authorities. The use of such data by the OECD is without prejudice to the status of the Golan Heights, East Jerusalem and Israeli settlements in the West Bank under the terms of international law.

Photo credits: Cover © 24Novembers

Corrigenda to OECD publications may be found on line at: *www.oecd.org/about/publishing/corrigenda.htm.*

Foreword

Financial reporting is one of the foundations of good fiscal management.

Against a backdrop of increased citizen demand, more open government, limited public spending capacity, and increasing efforts to achieve greater efficiency in delivering public services, high-quality financial reports are essential to ensure that governments make fiscal decisions based on up-to-date information and an accurate understanding of their financial position, and are the mechanism through which legislatures, auditors, and the public at large hold governments accountable for their financial performance.

Accordingly, the OECD - in collaboration with the International Federation of Accountants (IFAC) and Accountability. Now. Initiative - undertook a survey of selected financial reporting practices of OECD countries.

The *Survey* was sent to Ministries of Finance and equivalent bodies of all 34 OECD countries: Australia (AUS), Austria (AUT), Belgium (BEL), Canada (CAN), Chile (CHL), the Czech Republic (CZE), Denmark (DNK), Estonia (EST), Finland (FIN), France (FRA), Germany (DEU), Greece (GRC), Hungary (HUN), Iceland (ISL), Ireland (IRL), Israel (ISR), Italy (ITA), Japan (JPN), Korea (KOR), Luxembourg (LUX), Mexico (MEX), the Netherlands (NLD), New Zealand (NZL), Norway (NOR), Poland (POL), Portugal (PRT), the Slovak Republic (SVK), Slovenia (SVN), Spain (ESP), Sweden (SWE), Switzerland (CHE), Turkey (TUR), the United Kingdom (GBR), and the United States of America (USA). Answers from all 34 Ministries of Finance were collected from November 2015 to June 2016.

The Survey's results show that most OECD countries have reformed and modernised their financial reporting practices over the last decades.

Around three-quarters of OECD countries have adopted accrual accounting for their year-end financial reports as key priority. This means that governments' financial reporting is more comprehensive, with not only cash movements in and out of the government treasury reported to the public, but a range of other financial operations, as well as inventories of government' assets and liabilities.

Audit techniques and accounting standard setting mechanisms have also evolved significantly in the wake of accounting reforms. The adoption of accrual accounting often means that government publishes audited accounts, prepared in compliance with well-defined accounting standards.

The coverage of the accounts has also been extended by some countries.

While it is notable that governments still sought to improve the usefulness and understandability of their financial reports, a majority of OECD countries express satisfaction that greater transparency and accountability of their financial operations have been achieved following their accounting reforms.

Acknowledgements

This book is the result of the work undertaken for two decades by the OECD Financial Management Network and draws on surveys undertaken by the OECD since 2003 on accruals practices of its member countries. It is the product of sustained efforts of OECD countries' delegates for sharing insights on their accrual reform experiences.

This study was co-ordinated by Delphine Moretti from the OECD Budgeting and Public Expenditures Division, under the supervision of Jón Blöndal, together with Vincent Tophoff, Lead, Accountability. Now. Initiative of the International Federation of Accountants (IFAC).

Abdul Khan produced a detailed analysis of the survey's results.

Individual country profiles benefited from useful comments from Finance Ministries' officials.

This project also benefited from the active participation in meetings of delegates from the OECD Senior Budget Officials (SBO) Network.

Bonifacio Agapin, Hélène Leconte-Lucas and Lyora Raab are warmly thanked for providing invaluable assistance in the organisation of the meetings and workshops of the OECD Financial Management Network and editorial support.

Table of contents

Executive summary

The 2016 OECD Accruals Survey ("the Survey"), realised in partnership with the International Federation of Accountants and the *Accountability. Now.* initiative, takes a broad look at accrual reforms, by analysing not only accounting practices but also budgeting, consolidation, accounting standard setting, and external audit practices. In the wake of two decades of accrual reforms in OECD countries, this Survey is the first to gather feedback from all member countries' finance ministries on the rationale for deciding to move, or not, to accruals, implementation challenges, and perceived reform outcomes.

The results of the Survey show that around three-quarters of OECD countries have adopted accrual accounting for their year-end financial reports, although they have not necessarily implemented all aspects of what may be regarded as a full accrual accounting framework.

In particular, countries have progressed differently in populating their balance sheets. Most countries that have implemented accrual accounting reforms report a large range of assets, including land and buildings, defence equipment, and infrastructure, but certain liabilities, such as debt related to public-private partnerships (PPPs) and civil service pensions, are not reported by a significant number of countries. Surprisingly, natural resources are reported and measured by a minority of countries. The rationale for this situation varies depending on the country: some countries mention technical difficulties for inventorying assets and evaluating liabilities, while others indicate that these items are not reported because of the lack of international consensus on the appropriate accounting treatment.

More than a quarter of OECD countries prepare their annual budgets on an accrual basis. The survey does not, however, provide evidence of shared understanding and practices about the definition and meaning of accrual budgeting in terms of content and presentation of budgets and the nature of appropriations. In some countries, accrual budgets do not comprise a balance sheet and accrual-basis appropriations are used for current expenditures while capital expenditures remain accounted for on a cash basis.

The use of cash appropriations in a large majority of countries, including some of those that are using accrual budgeting to measure the impact of current and new public policies, suggests that governments are wary of the volatility and discretion in accrual valuations when it comes to control over resources spent by ministries and departments.

Looking at the accounting and budgeting framework as a whole, there are therefore two dominant practices: a vast majority of countries prepare accrual financial statements but use cash appropriations in their budgets.

Despite a majority of countries having adopted accrual accounting, the direct adoption of international accounting standards such as International Public Sector Accounting Standards (IPSAS) or International Financial Reporting Standards (IFRS) by national governments remains very low. Countries seem to favour national standards for accommodating a number of specific deviations. However, more than one-third of standard setters (in most cases, the finance ministry or an independent standard-setting board) use IPSAS or IFRS as primary or explicit references for developing their national standards.

Only 15% of OECD countries provide an overview of the public sector as a whole in their financial statements, and another 20% do so at the federal level. Few countries report that they plan to expand the coverage of their financial statements across levels of government. This may be due to constitutional provisions on the independence of local governments, the technical and practical challenges of consolidation, and a lack of appreciation of the need to use the full view of public finances in financial statements.

Financial statements are subject to independent external control or audit in all OECD countries, but only 62% of respondents indicated that their supreme audit institution provides an opinion on the year-end financial report according to international auditing standards. Among this group of countries, a high proportion of the audit opinions are qualified.

A majority of OECD countries have completed their public sector accounting reform programmes. Despite variations in the timescale, duration, and cost of reforms, countries encountered many similar challenges for preparing and implementing accrual accounting, including capacity building, establishing an inventory and valuation of assets and liabilities, the design and roll-out of new IT systems, and preparation of consolidated fiscal reports.

A majority of countries have expressed satisfaction that the reforms' transparency and accountability objectives have been fully achieved. Other objectives are not yet fully met by a majority of respondents. In particular, the use of full accrual costs for evaluating the management and performance of government entities is not widespread.

A number of countries, including early adopters of accrual accounting and/or budgeting, note that policy-makers and the general public have limited interest in accrual financial information. One obvious explanation for this situation is that, in many countries, the cash budget balance and net lending remain the key fiscal figures or targets and, consequently, the focus of most of the political debate.

As these issues undermine otherwise successful accruals reforms, several initiatives are ongoing to address them. For example, to make financial statements more user-friendly, governments have started publishing management commentaries and simplifying the notes and disclosures in the financial statements.

Chapter 1

Analysing and comparing country practices *

This Chapter compares and analyses the accounting basis for government year-end financial reports and budgets, audit techniques, accounting standard setting, and consolidation practices. It also discusses the design of recent accounting reforms, implementation challenges, the strategies and measures to address them, and the benefits expected and achieved.

*The analysis and comparison of countries practices was published in the OECD Journal on Budgeting, Vol. 16/1 (DOI: 10.1787/budget-16-5jlv2jx2mtzq) as part of the OECD, IFAC and Accountability. Now. Initiative collaboration.

The statistical data for Israel are supplied by and under the responsibility of the relevant Israeli authorities. The use of such data by the OECD is without prejudice to the status of the Golan Heights, East Jerusalem and Israeli settlements in the West Bank under the terms of international law.

Accounting in OECD countries

Accounting basis

This section discusses the accounting basis for government year-end financial reports. Historically, government fiscal reports used to be prepared mainly on a cash basis under which revenues and expenditures were included in financial reports when the related cash was received or paid. Over the last 25 years or so, however, governments - notably in OECD countries - have been moving toward the accrual accounting basis. Under this basis, revenues and expenses are reported when they are earned or incurred, regardless of the timing of the related cash receipts and payments.

The results of the survey show that annual financial reports are established on an accrual basis in the bulk of OECD countries (Figure 1):

- Twenty-five countries (73%) identify their annual financial reports as being based on accrual accounting.[1] This figure is to be compared with results of the first OECD Accruals Survey, dating back to 2003: At that date, only a quarter of countries reported using an accrual accounting system. The accrual accounting frameworks of countries take a number of forms. At one end of the spectrum are countries (such as New Zealand) that have embraced accrual as the basis for fiscal policy, budgeting, financial management, and reporting. At the other end, others (such as Japan) produce accrual-based financial statements as supplementary information to the cash-based accounts. In between, there are countries that produce accrual-based annual financial statements as their main or official accounts - not supplementary information - in addition to producing cash-based reports to show compliance with cash budgets.

- Another three countries (9%) indicated that they are in the process of transitioning to accrual accounting.[2] Moving from cash to accrual accounting is usually a lengthy and complex process. While the reforms are being implemented, governments may commence reporting some items on an accrual basis, while others continue to be reported on a cash basis. Therefore, at any point in time, some governments' financial reports may not fall neatly under either the cash or the accrual accounting category.

- Six countries (18%) indicated that they follow cash accounting.[3] Among this group, two countries indicated that they are considering whether to require ministries and departments (Ireland) and agencies (Norway) to report on an accrual basis in addition to continuing to report on a cash basis; Two countries (Italy and Luxembourg) have an ongoing reform process to move to accrual accounting, though progress has been limited. Only two countries (Germany and the Netherlands) indicated that they do not have any plans to adopt accruals, although one (the Netherlands) has agencies reporting on an accrual basis.

Figure 1. OECD Countries: Accounting basis for Annual Financial Reports

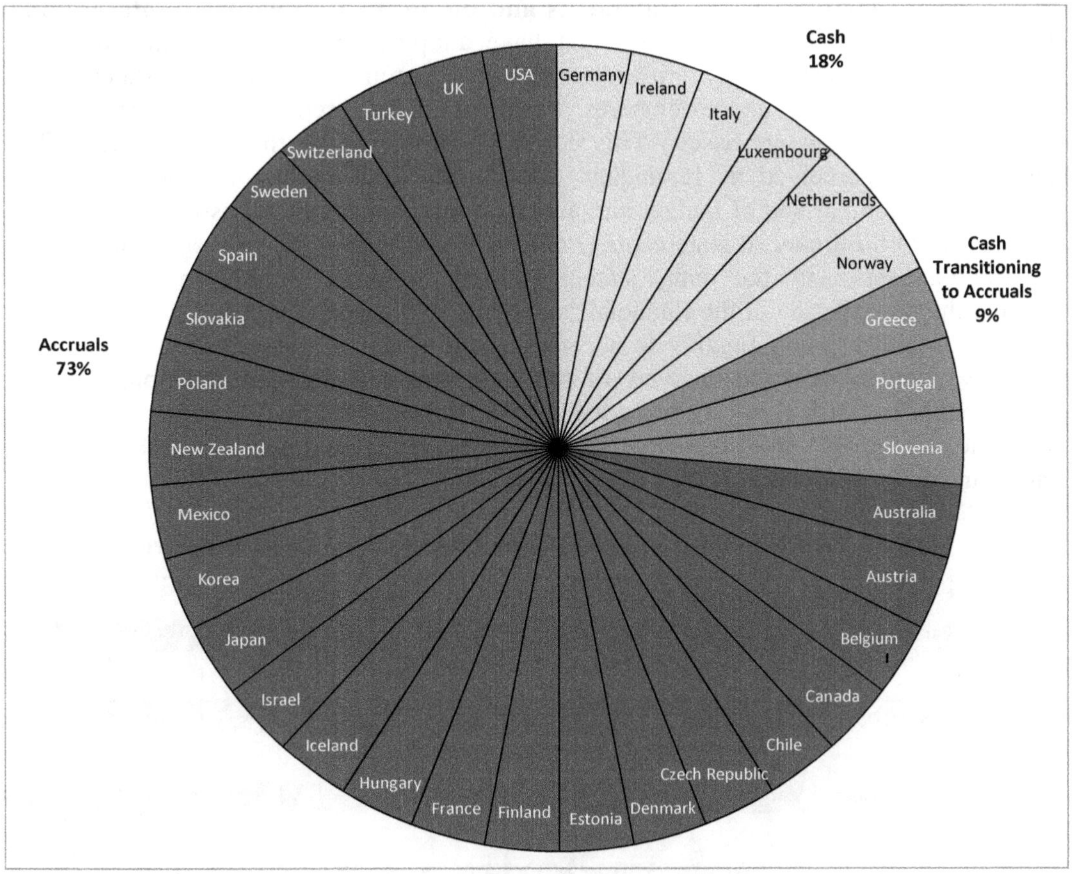

Notes: The figure above (and the following figures) reflects the answers provided by countries unless stated otherwise.

Countries that answered as having both accrual financial statements and cash financial reports (Czech Republic and Hungary) are classified as "Accruals."

Although Luxembourg is currently using a modified cash accounting system and has, therefore, been classified as "Cash," it is planning a transition to accrual accounting (see Figure 7).

Source: OECD Accruals Survey (2016).

Presentation of Annual Financial Reports

This section discusses the presentation of the annual financial report, and identifies which statements (balance sheet, income statement, cash flows, changes in net assets, comparison of budget and actuals) and comments (disclosures and management commentary) governments establish at year end. The presentation of financial reports is important because it affects the comprehensiveness and understandability of annual financial reports.

Countries that are following cash accounting or are transitioning to accruals establish only one primary statement at year end. This group of countries provides either a comparison of budget and actuals or a cash-flow statement with notes. Half of them also produce a simplified or incomplete balance sheet and income statement as supplementary information to budget outturn reports (Germany, Greece, Ireland, Portugal, and Slovenia).

More information is provided in accrual-basis financial reports, although they do not always include all key statements and disclosures required by international standards (Figure 2). All countries that have adopted accrual accounting prepare a balance sheet (or statement of financial position), income statement (or statement of financial performance), and disclosures. Fewer countries prepare a statement of cash flows and changes in net assets. This could be explained by the fact that cash-flow statements are perceived as redundant when other cash reports are presented - in particular the comparison of budget and actuals - and changes in net assets are disclosed in the notes to the financial statements (France). It might also reflect a concern with not overloading users with too many statements and, therefore, simplifying as much as possible the presentation of the financial statements in the public sector. Less than half of countries establish a commentary to accompany the financial report.[4] This may suggest that they consider that the analysis of the government's financial position, financial performance, and cash flows are provided at other stages of the budget process. Countries that indicated they do not establish a comparison of budget and actuals in their financial statements do so in separate budget execution reports.

Figure 2. OECD Countries: Presentation of Annual Financial Statements

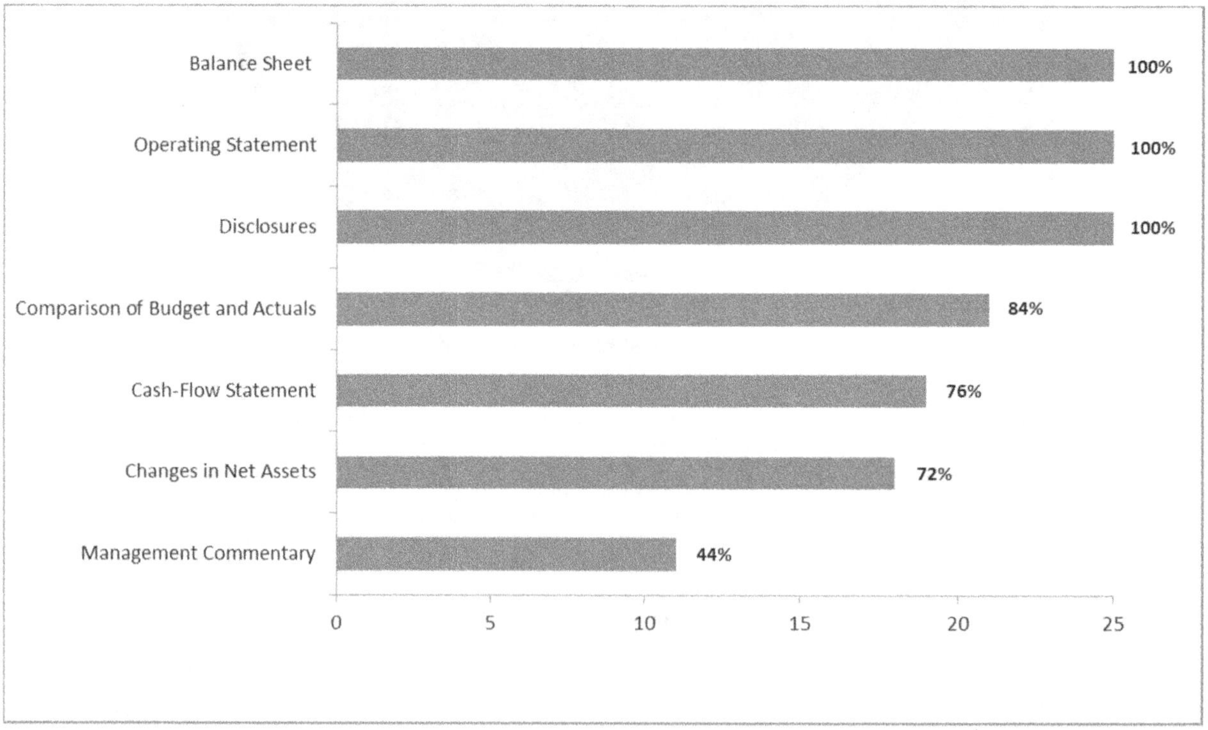

Source: OECD Accruals Survey (2016), based on the answers of the 25 countries implementing accrual accounting.

Box 1: Improving the Presentation of Financial Reports

Cash-flow statements, albeit not always included in government financial statements, are an integral part of accrual-based financial statements and are mandatory under internationally accepted accounting standards for both the private and the public sector.

Where governments prepare budgets on a cash basis but financial statements on an accrual basis, the cash-flow statement may provide a link between the cash-based budget execution reports and the accrual-based financial statements. Such a link, and the relevant reconciliations, are also key to facilitating an understanding, and encouraging the use, of accrual-based financial statements in a cash-based budgeting environment.

A cash-flow statement is also important where governments prepare accrual-based budgets, as in such cases the cash-flow statement provides essential information about the cash implications of the accrual budget, including the extent to which the policies and programmes are financed by the cash generated through taxation and other revenues rather than from borrowing.

As a matter of good practice, cash-based annual financial reports should, at a minimum, provide complete information about the cash resources of the governments. This would entail providing comprehensive information about all cash receipts and payments, appropriately classified. The net of the receipts and payments should be clearly reconciled with the cash balances at the beginning and end of the year.

International standards, such as IPSAS, IFRS, and Government Finance Statistics Manual (GFSM) 2014, provide formats for cash-flow statements, which governments could adopt or use as a guide.

Countries should also provide management commentary and analyses to make financial statements more accessible to users. Commentary and analyses are helpful to explain the financial performance and position, major variances between budgeted and actual amounts, major differences between current and prior years' amounts, achievement of service delivery and other performance objectives, and major risks and uncertainties that affect the public finances.

Countries could usefully consider supplementing the financial statements with a "citizens' guide" or similar explanatory materials to help explain the salient features of financial statements. Several countries covered by this survey provide excellent examples of such reports*.

* Note: See, for example, *A Citizen's Guide to the 2015 Financial Report of the U.S. Government*

Content of Annual Financial Reports

This section discusses the content of the annual financial report, covering assets, liabilities, expenses or expenditures, revenues, and financial commitments. It allows the assessment of whether governments provide a complete picture of their financial operations and their impact on the financial position, whether annual financial reports facilitate the discharge of accountability, and to provide the basis for informed decision making. The extent to which these objectives are achieved depends greatly on the content of financial reports. The accounting basis influences, to a significant extent, the content of financial reports. For example, under accrual accounting, assets and liabilities are required to be recognised, measured, and reported in accordance with specified accounting policies and principles. Under cash accounting, this is not a requirement, although some countries may report some of this information, as discussed below.

Countries reporting on a cash basis generally provide financial information that is not restricted solely to cash transactions. All but one of the six countries reporting on a cash basis provide information on cash balances, debt, guarantees, and commitments. This would suggest that countries reporting on a cash basis acknowledge the need for inventorying and measuring assets and liabilities. Some countries also keep track of the stock and value of a number of other assets and liabilities. Germany and Norway, in particular, disclose the value of selected assets and liabilities. Norway also discloses the value of its natural resources, albeit in the budget. Ireland provides, as supplementary information, an operating cost statement and a balance sheet, Italy has a separate document that provides information about assets and liabilities, and the Netherlands account for interest on an accrual basis in an otherwise cash-based framework. The three countries transitioning to accrual accounting supply additional information on accrued expenses and tax receivables (Greece, Slovenia), or fixed assets (Portugal).

Box 2: Importance of commitments and guarantees

Commitments are explicit or implicit agreements to make payment(s) to another party in exchange for operating or capital goods and services. Commitments may be related to specific goods and services and arise from a formal action, e.g., the issuance of a purchase order or the signing of a contract. Commitments can also be of an ongoing type that requires a series of payments over an indeterminate period of time and may or may not involve a contract, e.g., salaries, utilities, and entitlement payments. Commitments are usually incurred when governments enter into contractual or other arrangements with third parties. This is followed by the receipt of goods or services when a liability arises.

Keeping track of commitments is important in public sector financial reporting because their control is essential for effective expenditure control. Once contracts have been entered into (i.e., a commitment has been created), it may be, in practice, difficult to avoid the liability. Therefore, a sound expenditure control system needs to focus on commitment controls (i.e., control before commitments are entered into through contracts, purchase orders, or other arrangements) regardless of the basis of financial reporting or budgeting.

Guarantees are formal assurances of specified actions and/or outcome. In the public sector, governments usually provide guarantees for the debt of third parties, including state-owned entities. Governments can also provide guarantees to private sector parties (e.g., to make up for any specified losses due to a demand shortfall in the context of a purchaser provider partnership arrangement). During the recent global financial crisis, many governments had to provide extremely large guarantees to save vulnerable private sector organisations, mainly financial institutions. Even in the absence of a financial crisis, guarantees can be a significant part of a government's contingent liabilities and should be disclosed in financial reports together with other major fiscal risks.

Countries that report on an accrual basis have progressed differently in populating their balance sheet with assets and liabilities (Table 1). All countries report their financial liabilities and assets, as well as accrued expenses. Other elements are reported in a less consistent way:

- A majority of countries that have adopted accrual accounting disclose land and buildings (92%), infrastructure (92%), tax receivables (85%), defence assets and inventories (79%), and derivatives (75%). This suggests that operational issues for inventorying and measuring these items have been overcome. However, remaining difficulties are evidenced by the relatively large number of financial statements that received a qualified audit opinion due to issues with the reporting of fixed assets (see below).

- For civil and military service pension liabilities, practices vary greatly: 39% of countries record them on the balance sheet, 14% disclose them in the notes, and 36% do not disclose them at all. Among these last two groups of countries, some countries consider that their employees - civil or military - do not have any contractual pension entitlements.5

Similar reasons are mentioned for not reporting social benefits (53% of countries do not report them).[6] The lack of reference accounting treatment in international standards can also explain this situation.[7]

Some countries mentioned that the sustainability of their pensions and social benefits policies was assessed in their *Long-Term Fiscal Sustainability Report* (also called *Intergenerational Report*). This report assesses both future liabilities and taxation to fund the liabilities, comparing future revenues and spending and therefore highlighting possible fiscal imbalances, rather than doing this in the balance sheet.

- With regards to Public-Private Partnerships (PPPs), 36% of countries do not report these assets and liabilities on the balance sheet. This could be explained by technical difficulties for inventorying contracts and evaluating the related debt, or implementing the control approach required by international standards. Similarly to what was mentioned for pensions and social benefits, there might be a reluctance to report on potentially significant amounts of debt related to these contracts.

- Natural resources and heritage assets are reported respectively by 11% and 43% of governments, which could be explained by the lack of reference accounting treatment in these areas, and difficulties for establishing reliable and meaningful valuations. The other reason, for countries such as Australia, is that the federal government is not responsible for natural resources, which are the responsibility of state jurisdictions.

Table 1. OECD countries: Reporting practices for of selected assets and liabilities in Annual Financial Statements

	Balance Sheet	Disclosure	Not Reported	N/A
Tax Receivables	AUS, AUT, CAN, CHL, CZE, DNK, EST, FRA, GRC, HUN, ISL, ISR, JPN, KOR, NZL, POL, SVK, SVN, ESP, SWE, CHE, TUR, GBR, USA	BEL, MEX,	FIN, PRT	
Natural Resources	ISR, SVN, SWE	EST, USA	AUS, AUT, CAN, CHL, CZE, FIN, GRC, HUN, ISL, KOR, MEX, NZL, POL, PRT, ESP, CHE, TUR, GBR	BEL, DNK, FRA, JPN, SVK
Land Buildings	AUS, AUT, BEL, CAN, CHL, CZE, DNK, EST, FIN, FRA, HUN, ISR, JPN, KOR, MEX, NZL, POL, PRT, SVK, SVN, ESP, SWE, CHE, TUR, GBR, USA		GRC, ISL	

Table 1. OECD countries: Reporting practices for of selected assets and liabilities in Annual Financial Statements *(cont.)*

Infrastructure Assets, excluding PPPs	AUS, AUT, BEL, CAN, CZE, DNK, EST, FIN, FRA, HUN, ISR, JPN, KOR, MEX, NZL, POL, PRT, SVK, SVN, ESP, SWE, CHE, TUR, GBR, USA		CHL, GRC, ISL	
PPP Assets and Liabilities	AUS, AUT, CAN, DNK, EST, FIN, FRA, ISR, JPN, KOR, NZL, POL, SVK, TUR, GBR, USA	CZE, HUN, MEX, ESP	BEL, CHL, GRC, ISL, PRT, SVN,	SWE, CHE
Heritage Assets	AUS, AUT, CAN, CZE, FIN, FRA, NZL, POL, SVN, ESP, SWE, GBR	ISR, KOR, USA	BEL, CHL, DNK, GRC, HUN, ISL, MEX, PRT, CHE, TUR	EST, JPN, SVK
Defence Assets and Inventories	AUS, AUT, BEL, CAN, CZE, DNK, EST, FRA, HUN, ISR, JPN, MEX, NZL, POL, PRT, SVK, SVN, ESP, SWE, TUR, GBR, USA		CHL, FIN, GRC, ISL, KOR, CHE	
Derivatives	AUS, AUT, BEL, CHL, CZE, DNK, EST, FIN, FRA, ISR, JPN, KOR, NZL, SVK, SVN, ESP, SWE, CHE, TUR, GBR, USA	CAN, HUN	GRC, ISL, PRT	MEX, POL
Civil and Military Service Pensions	AUS, CAN, EST, ISR, ISL, KOR, NZL, SVK, SWE, GBR, USA	AUT, FIN, FRA, CHE	BEL, CHL, CZE, DNK, GRC, MEX, PRT, SVN, ESP, TUR	HUN, JPN, POL
Social Benefits	CAN, EST, FRA, ISR, JPN, NZL, POL, PRT, SVK	HUN, USA	AUS, AUT, BEL, CHL, DNK, FIN, GRC, ISL, KOR, MEX, ESP, SWE, CHE, TUR, GBR	CZE, SVN

Source: OECD Accruals Survey (2016), based on the answers of the 28 countries that report on accrual or cash transitioning to accrual basis.

Preparation basis for budgets in OECD countries

This section discusses the preparation basis for budgets. While a budget is prepared on the basis of a range of concepts and principles, for the purposes of this report the term "preparation basis of budgets" has been used to refer to the basis on which the financial implications of the budget policies and programmes are measured and reported in the budget. This section also discusses Parliamentary appropriations, which in some countries are distinct from the "budget."[8] They are defined for the purpose of this report as "authorisation by an act of parliament to permit government entities to incur obligations, and/or to pay for them from the treasury," even though the definition of appropriations may differ between countries.

A majority of OECD countries prepare their budgets on cash or modified cash basis (Figure 3.a):

- Twenty-one countries (or 62%) use the cash basis for preparing the budget and appropriations. Within that group, however, many countries provide information on debt, commitments, and guarantees in the budget and, therefore, do not qualify their system as "cash basis" per se. In particular, commitments are considered as a special feature of budget systems that do not fall neatly into the cash or accrual categories.9 In this group, one country (Luxembourg) plans to adopt accrual budgeting over the medium term.

- Three countries (or 9%) prepare budgets comprising some items budgeted on an accrual basis: This group of countries has been designated as "Cash and Accrual."10 Among this group, one country (Estonia) is well advanced in its preparatory work for a move to full accrual budgeting commencing with the 2017 budget. Other countries have indicated that, despite forecasting some elements of their budget on an accrual basis, they did not contemplate a transition to accrual budgeting.

- Ten countries (or 29%) have adopted the accrual basis for the preparation of their budgets. A majority of countries within that group presents a full set of prospective financial statements (Australia, Canada, Denmark, New Zealand, Switzerland, and the United Kingdom). Other countries establish incomplete or simplified versions of the financial statements (Austria, Iceland, Chile, and Mexico).

Accrual budgeting does not entail a systematic use of accrual appropriations (Figure 3.b). Among the countries that use accrual budgeting, two (New Zealand and the United Kingdom) use full accrual appropriations.[11] Other countries within that group mix accrual and cash appropriations (Australia, Austria, Denmark, Iceland, and Switzerland), or use cash appropriations only (Canada, Chile, Mexico). This would suggest that countries may be wary of the volatility and discretion in accruals valuations (in particular with regard to provisions and depreciations), and believe that cash appropriations allow a better control over resources spent by ministries and departments, even when they are using accrual forecasts to measure the impact of current and new public policies.

Appropriations are used for authorising current and capital expenditures in a large majority of countries. All countries authorise annually the capital and current expenses or expenditures.[12] In more than half of countries, authorisations are also granted for incurring commitments. Three countries (Australia, Iceland, and the UK) indicate that Parliament also grants an annual authorisation for incurring pension liabilities.

Figure 3. OECD Countries: Selected budgeting practices

a. Preparation basis for budgets

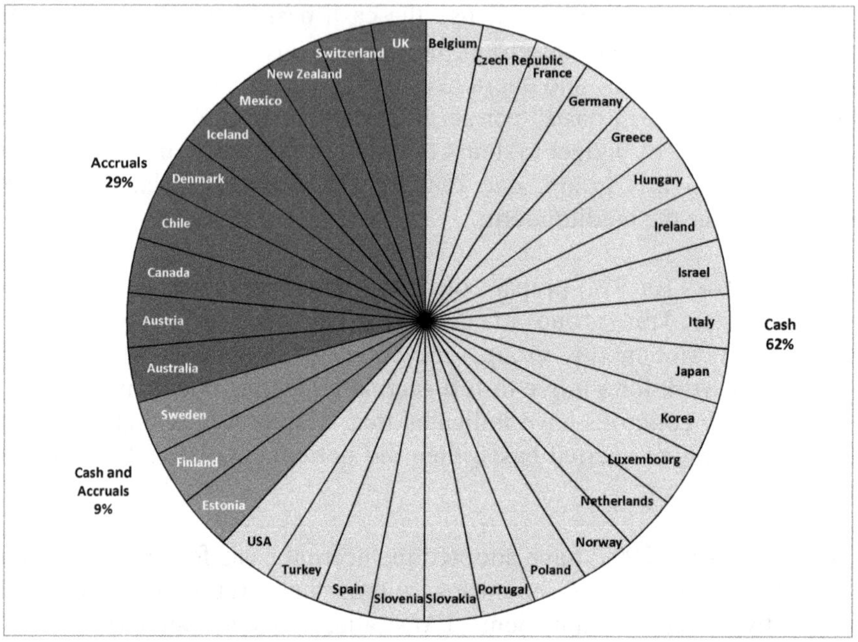

b. Nature of appropriations

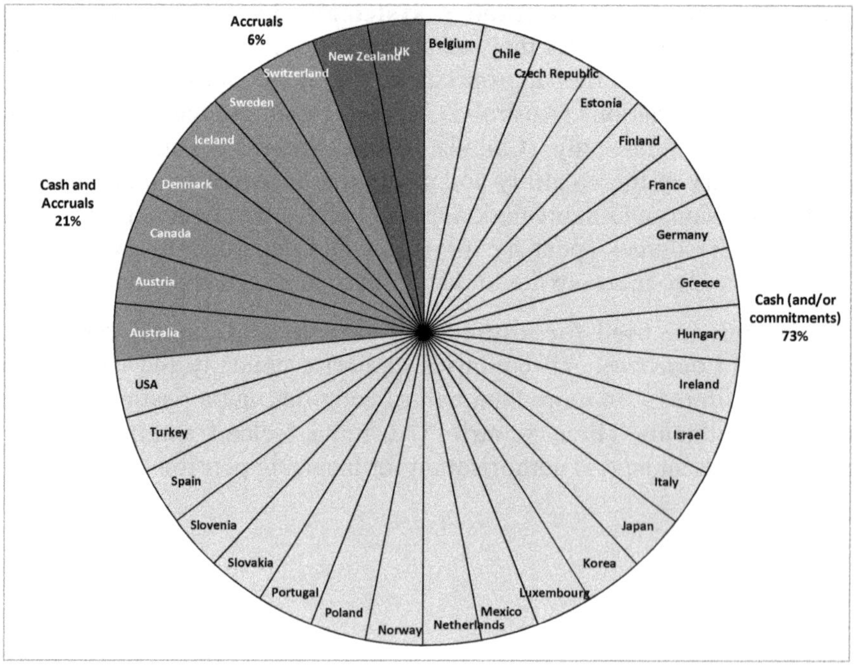

Note: Sweden and Finland are presented (Figure 3.a) in the "Cash and Accruals" category as the budget includes both accrual and cash elements, Estonia is planning a transition to accrual accounting to be completed by 2017.

Source: OECD Accruals Survey (2016).

Overall, the survey draws a varied picture of budgeting practices. Budgeting is indeed an area where, contrary to accounting, standards or generally accepted principles have not yet been developed, and practices are related to the ways the Parliament authorises and controls public spending, and the nature of the national fiscal targets and rules. Categorising budget frameworks between cash and accrual, therefore, proves difficult - these are accounting concepts that may not fully reflect the specificities of budget practices.

Looking at the accounting and budgeting framework as a whole, there are three broad models (Table 2). Half of the countries (50%) prepare accrual financial statements and cash budgets and budget execution reports. A third of countries (32%) prepare accrual financial statements and budgets, the latter incorporating either accrual, or cash, or both accrual and cash appropriations and related budget execution reports. The remaining countries (18%) prepare cash budgets and cash financial reports.

Table 2. OECD Countries: Accounting basis for Annual Financial Reports and preparation basis for budgets

	Countries
Accrual Financial Statements and Budgets [1]	AUS, AUT, CAN, CHE, CHL, DNK, EST, GBR, ISL, MEX, NZL
Accrual Financial Statements and Cash Budgets [2]	BEL, CZE, ESP, GRC, FIN, FRA, HUN, ISR, JPN, KOR, POL PRT, SVK, SVN, SWE, TUR, USA
Cash Financial Reports and Budget	DEU, IRL, ITA, LUX, NLD, NOR

Notes: 1) Includes Estonia, which is transitioning to accrual budgeting in 2017; 2) includes countries with cash transitioning to accrual financial statements (GRE, POR, and SVN) and budgets comprising cash and accrual elements (SWE and FIN).

Source: OECD Accruals Survey (2016), based on the answers of the 28 countries that report on accrual or cash transitioning to accrual basis.

Fiscal Reports' Institutional Coverage

This section discusses the institutional coverage of fiscal reports. As fiscal activity is carried out by different levels of government, this section discusses what public sector entities are part of budgets and financial reports, and whether fiscal reports provide a full understanding of the amount and composition of public spending and revenue, and the related accumulation of government assets and liabilities.

Regardless of the accounting basis, very few countries present a full overview of the public finances across all levels of government in their financial statements (Figure 4). At one end of the spectrum, five (or 14%) countries establish financial statements that encompass the central and local levels of government, as well as state-owned corporations; another eight (or 24%) require financial statements that cover all entities over which the national or federal government exercises authority (control). At the other end of the spectrum, ten (or 29%) countries cover only the budgetary entities in their annual financial statements. Within that group, several countries provide supplementary information to the public and Parliament. For example, Portugal presents a number of aggregated figures in the year-end financial statements for the regional and local governments.

The variety of practices used for consolidation is explained by both the consolidation criterion and national circumstances:

- A majority of countries indicate that the scope of their financial statements is defined by law. In this group of countries, local and regional governments are more often included in the consolidated financial statements than in countries that follow the "control" criterion for consolidation.
- About one-quarter of respondents use "control" as their consolidation criterion. In this group of countries, local and regional governments, or social security funds, may not be consolidated in the government's financial statements because they are constitutionally or legally independent.
- Some countries mentioned technical or operational difficulties as factors explaining the limited coverage of their financial statements.
- Finally, some countries mentioned that the full view of public finances was provided in fiscal statistics, and questioned the need and use of such information in financial statements.

Figure 4. OECD Countries: Institutional coverage in Annual Financial Report

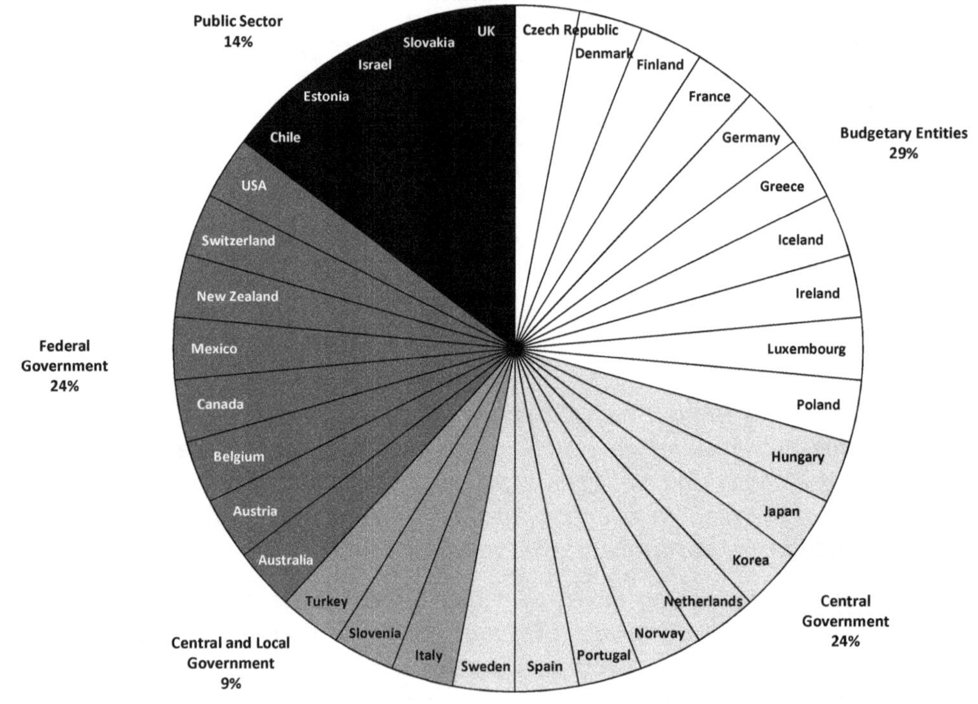

Note: Some of the countries classified in the category "Central Government" have specified that their financial statements include the Social Security Funds (HUN, NLD, NOR, PRT, ESP); countries classified in the category "Central and Local Governments" include the Social Security Funds; Iceland's financial statements will present going forward a consolidated view of the public sector as required by the Organic Budget Law adopted in 2015.

Source: OECD Accruals Survey (2016).

In a majority of countries, financial statements have broader coverage than the budget. Most of the governments that prepare consolidated financial statements do not establish budgets with a similar coverage.[13] The few countries that have aligned the coverage of fiscal reports, notably the United Kingdom[14] and New Zealand, consider that harmonisation is beneficial for a number of reasons, including producing consistent and comparable figures that are believed to be more transparent, understandable, and easier to use. Where the coverage is not aligned, this likely reflects the fact that the budget and financial statements do not serve the same purpose: While the budget is mainly the vehicle legislatures use for deciding how expenditures should be allocated, financial statements provide a more global view of the financial situation of the public sector, including public corporations and sub-national governments in certain cases.

Consolidation concepts and practices vary between countries. The concept of consolidation is understood differently by countries: Certain countries consider entities that receive transfers disclosed in the government's budget, or entities reported at equity value in the balance sheet, as "consolidated" in the budget or financial statement. For those countries that do undertake a consolidation according to international standards,[15] some establish consolidated financial statements by "sub-sectors" (Slovak Republic, for example). About half of the countries rely on a harmonised chart of accounts, while another half uses consolidation packages or templates to gather information necessary for consolidation purposes. Most governments use an automated integrated financial management information system (IFMIS) to prepare the consolidation. It should be noted that there are continuing problems in this area as evidenced by the relatively large number of financial statements that received a qualified audit opinion due to the issues with intra-group eliminations, as explained in the following section.

Standard Setting and Auditing[16]

Standard-Setting

This section discusses the various practices for setting accounting standards. Financial accounting standards - also referred to as reporting standards - define how financial statements are to be prepared and specific items are to be identified, recognised, valued, and reported in financial statements. Governments may set standards directly (e.g., through the Ministries of Finance, MoF) or create independent standard-setting authorities. Regardless of the standard-setting process, the accounting standards may be specific to the country, or derived from international standards. Understanding these mechanisms is important to assess the level of quality and consistency of accounting practices in OECD countries.

The MoF is the standard-setting authority in about half of OECD countries (Figure 7a). The level of guidance on accounting principles and standards stipulated in the law varies according to countries. Where the legal framework defines only general principles, the MoF is in most cases tasked with setting the accounting standards, either directly (32% of cases) or in consultation with an advisory board (18% of countries). Independent national standard-setting boards are responsible for standard setting in a further 24% of countries (Australia, Canada, France, Israel, Mexico, New Zealand, and the USA).

Nearly all countries develop national accounting standards, but many use international frameworks as a reference (Figure 7b). Standards are established at the national level in all but one country, Switzerland, which is the only country that directly adopts IPSAS.[17] International standards (IFRS, IPSAS, or statistics frameworks[18]) are considered as an explicit or primary reference for developing national standards in 40% of the countries. Other countries often mention them as guidance. Countries seem to favour national standards for accommodating a number of specific deviations, such as limiting the quantity of disclosures (for example, Sweden), defining boundaries for the financial statements that are aligned with the ones used in the budget and the fiscal statistics (United Kingdom, Australia, or New Zealand), or reflecting the specificities of the national legal frameworks and public policies (France, for example, with regard to the accounting treatment for the public service pension system).

Figure 5. OECD countries: Accounting standard-setting authority and type of standards

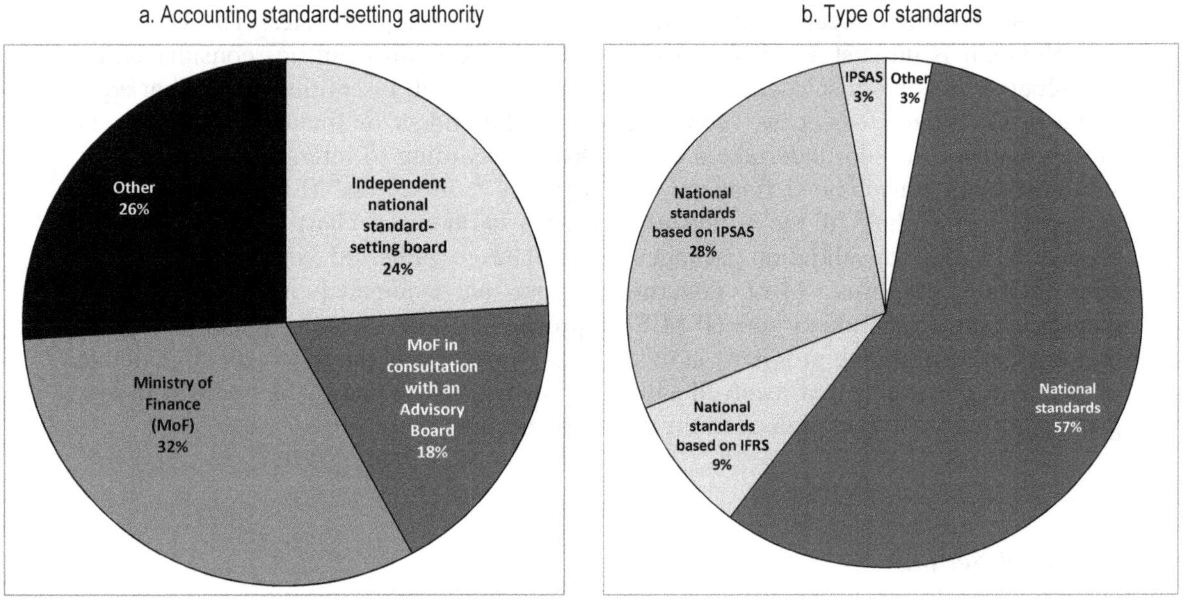

Note: In Figure 3.a, *other* is government (Belgium, Hungary, Ireland, Poland, Sweden, and Switzerland); Comptroller General of the Republic (Chile); and specific committee (Germany); in Figure 3.b, *other* is national standards based on European system of accounts (Belgium).

Source: OECD Accruals Survey (2016).

Auditing

This section discusses the types of external audits on annual financial reports. This function can be exercised by supreme audit institutions (SAIs), which are independent public institutions with a mandate for overseeing the management of public funds and the quality and credibility of the government's' reported financial data, or audit firms.

The annual financial reports are subject to some form of external audit in all OECD countries (Figure 6.a). A majority of respondents (56%) indicated that their SAIs follow international auditing standards and provide an opinion on whether the financial statements present a true and fair view.[19] Another group of countries declared that the financial statements are audited in accordance with national requirements set out in the constitution or laws, which in most cases require auditors to assess the compliance of annual expenditures with the Parliamentary authorisations and regulations on financial controls.

A high proportion of the audit opinions are qualified (Figure 6.b). Especially in the group of countries that prepare and publish financial statements according to international audit standards, a large majority of audit opinions are qualified. Issues with the inventory and valuation of fixed assets (in particular, defence equipment) and the general quality and reliability of accounting data lead to the qualifications in a majority of cases. Issues with boundaries of government financial reporting and intra-group eliminations are also mentioned by around half of countries, which may not fully reflect the scale of the challenges associated with consolidation, as few countries have started establishing consolidated financial statements. Continuing engagement and co-operation with the SAI is often mentioned by respondents as an important success factor for implementing accrual accounting and improving the reliability of the financial statements over time.

Figure 6. OECD countries: Type of audits and issues with year-end financial statements

a. Type of audits b. Nature of qualifications

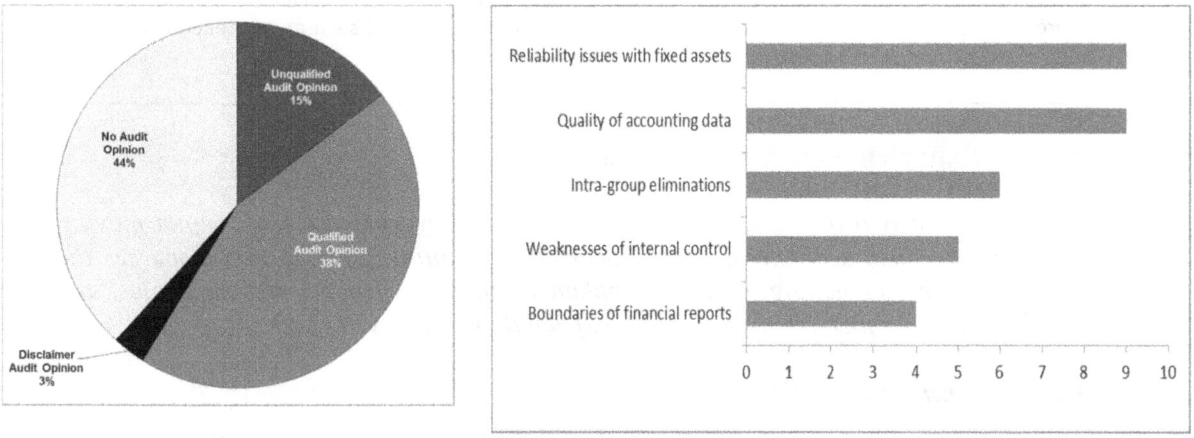

Note: Figure 6a: where no audit opinion is provided according to international auditing standards, SAIs carry out compliance audits or other types of assurance engagements; Figure 6b: for the 15 countries that have specified the sources of disclaimer or qualifications.

Source: OECD Accruals Survey (2016).

Box 3: Independent audit provides assurance of the quality of the financial statements

The importance of high-quality, independent audits as countries move toward accrual accounting cannot be overemphasised. As governments adopt accrual accounting, there will be an increasing need for skills and judgments to prepare financial statements. Accounting policies would need to be formulated, estimates would have to be made based on information that may be incomplete or subject to uncertainty, and a balance would need to be struck between the need for transparency and the volume and complexity of the information provided. Annual financial statements should also aim to provide a true and fair view.

All these factors make it particularly important that accrual-based financial statements are subject to audits to provide the necessary assurances to users that, among other things, the statements have been prepared with due care, are free from materials errors or misstatements, and comply with relevant standards and legal requirements. As well, auditors must have the requisite skills and follow auditing standards that are consistent with those issued by the International Organization of Supreme Audit Institutions (INTOSAI). It is also important that a country's constitution or laws guarantee the independence of the auditors to enable them to perform their duties free from undue influence.

Box 3: Independent audit provides assurance of the quality of the financial statements *(cont.)*

More attention should be directed to achieving unqualified audit opinions in accordance with international standards. The users of the financial statements need to have assurance that the financial statements present a true and fair view of a government's financial position (assets and liabilities), financial performance (revenues and expenses), and the cash flows. This will require a concerted effort to ensure that financial statements are prepared in accordance with IPSAS or comparable standards. It may also require efforts by the SAIs, aided by the parliament and the national executive, to improve their skills to undertake the audit of such financial statements.

The achievement of independent audits in accordance with international standards should be incorporated explicitly as a target in the planning of accrual reforms. Where a phased implementation approach is adopted, the audit aspect could also be phased in. For example, audits with specific scope limitations could be allowed in the earlier phases, while a full-scope audit could be included in a later or the final phase. Financial statements could also be subject to a period of trial audits to identify and address issues before full-scope audits are instituted. Australia adopted such an approach with the audit of the government's consolidated financial statements.

Accrual Reform Experiences in OECD Countries[20]

Over the past two decades, a growing number of governments have begun moving away from pure cash accounting toward accrual accounting. This section discusses the design of recent accounting reforms, implementation challenges, the strategies and measures to address them, and the benefits expected and achieved.

Where do countries stand?

A majority of countries stated that they have completed their reform programmes (Figure 9).[21] This highlights a major shift in public accounting practices since the 2000s, as only 24% of countries reported using accrual accounting in the first OECD Accruals Survey (2003). However, the objectives and scale of reforms vary significantly: The United Kingdom's reforms involved a transition to accruals for the whole of the public sector and the introduction of accrual budgeting, while France's reforms are aimed at implementing accrual accounting at the budgetary central government level only. In addition, as discussed earlier, the accrual frameworks show a great deal of variations. Another group of countries described their reforms as ongoing, some of them linked to the possible development of European Public Sector Accounting Standards (EPSAS). Few countries have neither implemented nor contemplated any accrual reform. The main reasons for this are the lack of political support, concern that the benefits are unlikely to exceed costs (Germany), and satisfaction that cash-based budgets and financial reports (with interest budgeted and accounted for on an accrual basis) provide all the necessary information (the Netherlands).

Figure 7. OECD countries: Status of accrual reforms

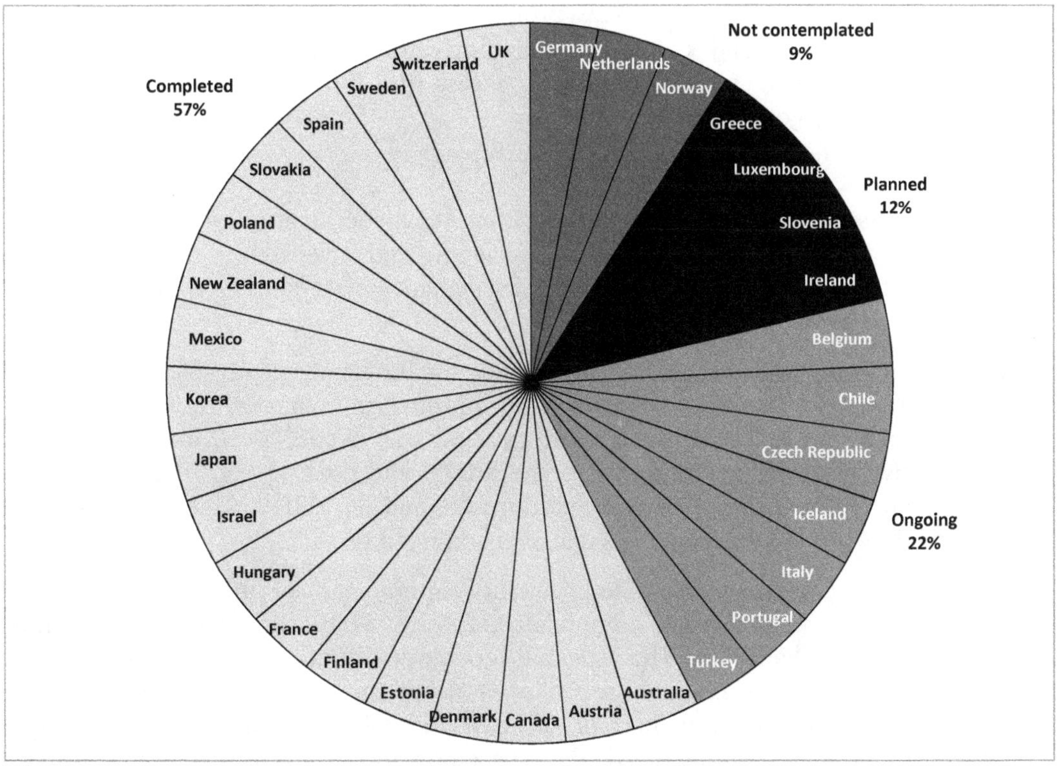

Source: OECD Accruals Survey (2016).

The adoption to accrual accounting was often part of, and intended to facilitate, wider public management reform initiatives. The motivation for reform mentioned most often in the survey were presenting a fair view of the public finances, assessing the full costs of government operations, introducing or enhancing a performance culture, and modernising public management. Other motivations for the reforms were mentioned as well, including:

Transparency and accountability:

- improving fiscal transparency and accountability;
- presenting a fair view of the public finances;
- promoting informed decision making; and
- meeting external reporting requirements.

Strategic resource management:

- providing information and analysis to the senior managers;
- helping the government translate its strategy into action;
- promoting informed decision making;
- strengthening the institutional capacity for budgeting, expenditure management, and the financial management of governmental operations;
- introducing or enhancing a performance orientation including policy evaluation; and
- making it easier to recruit skilled staff when government accounting standards are more comparable to those used in the private sector.

Improving awareness and management of costs:

- assessing the full costs of polices, programmes, and government operations,
- recording assets and liabilities, including infrastructure assets and employee entitlements that would also help assess the full magnitude of resources consumed by government; and
- measuring the result of operations of government entities.

Countries that have adopted accrual budgeting, or a combination of cash and accrual budgeting in addition to accrual accounting, mentioned consistency between *ex ante* (annual budgets) and *ex post* (annual financial statements) reports as a key motivating factor.

Most countries considered user needs to guide the design of reforms. The demand for relevant, reliable, and comprehensive financial information emanated from both internal management and external stakeholders. Information was needed by *i)* management and senior executives to facilitate planning, organisation, and control, and *ii)* external users including the parliament, foreign investors, Eurostat, and the IMF to assess the discharge of accountability and facilitate analysis and decision making.

The countries appreciated that, to meet the requirements of these users, financial reports would have to provide a comprehensive view of the government's revenues, expenses, assets, and liabilities. The financial reports would also need to have a broader coverage and provide information about the whole of the public sector, including the central and the local governments, or at least the whole of a particular level of government. Accrual accounting, particularly based on, or consistent with, internationally accepted standards was considered the means to achieve these ends.

The European Union initiative on harmonised EPSAS is causing some countries to consider reforms. Ireland - one of the few countries following cash accounting - is considering a possible move to accrual accounting for departments and offices in response to the EU developments and the recommendations of the IMF's fiscal transparency evaluation (FTE).[22] Ireland indicated that any move to accrual accounting will be progressed in line with developments at the EU level. Italy - another country currently following cash accounting - has taken some steps for a possible adoption of accrual accounting in response to the EU initiative. Luxembourg is undertaking preparatory work to prepare for a possible adoption of EPSAS.

The government or the MoF sponsored the reforms in a majority of countries. The MoFs (often through the budget office or the treasury) were the agencies responsible for the preparation, monitoring, and implementation of the reforms in most countries. Other sponsors of the reforms included government agencies such as the Office of the Comptroller General or the National Financial Management Authority.

The results of the survey do not allow evaluating precisely the duration and costs of the reforms. Costs seem to vary significantly depending on the scale of the IT systems upgrades and consulting services required, but only one country provided detailed information. In New Zealand, the public management reforms as a whole—of which accrual accounting and budgeting was only a part - cost an estimated NZD 160 - NZD 180 million, or 0.1% of expenses over the period of implementation.[23] Some countries noted that the IT systems were upgraded as part of the normal replacement/maintenance cycle and, therefore, did not generate any significant additional operating costs.

What Were Reform Challenges?

Countries seem to have experienced a number of common challenges for implementing reforms:

- The identification and valuation of assets and liabilities are considered as the most challenging tasks during the preparatory stage of the reforms. This is understandable because, in most cases, countries did not have reliable or complete records of assets - particularly non-financial assets - that were owned and identified, let alone the values of such assets. Similarly, the recognition and reporting of civil service and military pension liabilities, PPPs, etc., can present conceptual as well as valuation challenges. Based on their experience, countries suggest that, among other things, the complexity of the task should be recognised at the outset and entities should be allowed sufficient time to complete the task.

- Putting in place new IT systems presented challenges at the implementation phase in most countries. It was noted that the implementation of a new IT system is already difficult enough when the accounting framework remain unchanged. The challenges increase exponentially, however, when the accounting basis changes from cash to accrual and the new system is required to support this new framework. Determining the requirements of the IT systems early in the process was identified as a key critical success factor. Using commercial off-the-shelf systems and related business processes was also identified as a success factor.

- A number of countries also mentioned difficulties for realising changes in legislation, as these have to be discussed with the political leadership, the preparation of consolidated financial statements, and the preparation of financial statements within agreed timetable.

Most governments sequenced implicitly or explicitly the move to accrual accounting. Most governments have taken a realistic view of the time required to implement the reforms. A key strategy was to adopt a phased approach to the reforms in order to manage the challenges, to minimise the risk of failure, and maximise the probability of a successful implementation. Some countries (for example, Denmark) also included a pilot phase or limited test runs, during which lessons would be learnt prior to proceeding with full implementation. In most cases, the balance sheet was populated progressively. For example, in France, individual evaluations of defence assets were established a few years after the first publication of the government's balance sheet.

Effective project management and co-ordination and strong leadership by the MoF (or another central agency such as the budget office or the treasury) were identified as critical. Many countries underline the importance of providing sustained training and assistance to implementation units. Guidance and guidelines have also been used in all countries. Additionally, countries stressed the need to have smaller project teams or groups responsible for specific tasks, such as legal and regulatory changes, developing guidance and training materials, developing and implementing IT systems, and preparing financial statements.

The importance of human resources management and capacity building was a common theme. In particular, countries stressed the importance of having staff or consultants with knowledge and experience of accrual accounting, IT systems, and consolidation to address the biggest challenges they faced. Indeed, a number of countries, for example Canada, which successfully implemented a sophisticated accrual accounting framework, indicated that, at the time of the commencement of the reforms, many finance personnel had never been exposed to accrual concepts. Therefore, training programmes were delivered in all countries, and experts were often hired to supplement the existing skills base.

Table 3. OECD countries: Strategies and measures to address the reform challenges

Major Challenges	Strategies and Measures
Adapting existing laws and regulations	• Working collaboratively with the political level, and obtaining cross-party support for legislative changes. • Establishing special units to deal with the legal and regulatory issues
Design, development, and implementation of IT systems	• Strong project management • Using consultants/experts with specialist skills and technical knowledge • Developing requirements (e.g., conceptual design and functional requirements) of the system at an early stage. • Leveraging off corporate systems and practices
Identification and valuation of assets and liabilities as part of the opening balance sheet	• Consultation with, and engagement of, the appropriate departments early in the process. • Development of a model for costing capital assets where no records exist for actual historical cost. • Adopting a phased approach and allowing more time to ministries and departments • Coordinated effort by preparers and auditors.
Developing guidance and training materials and delivering training	• Establishing dedicated team(s) • Training existing staff and hiring people with subject matter skills and experience • Training existing staff • Quality assurance of training materials
Preparing consolidated financial statements	• Role of experienced and qualified staff critical • Effective coordination with entities to be consolidated • Adopting a phased approach—starting with a few eliminations
Preparing financial statements in a timely manner	• Strong project management and coordination • Role of experienced and qualified staff critical
Preparing for audit requirements and addressing audit qualifications	• Auditor relationship management and communication
Estimating, monitoring, and controlling the costs of the reforms	• Effective project management

Were Reform Objectives Achieved?

Countries that engage in accruals reform pursue a broad range of objectives, such as enhanced accountability, increased transparency toward the public at large, more political and public awareness about the state of public finances, better information on full costs of operations, increased efficiency of the administration's business processes, more informed decisions about asset and liability management, and producing meaningful figures and financial analysis.

Overall, satisfaction that reforms objectives have been achieved is mixed (Table 3). Ministries of Finance in around half of the countries considered that the expected benefits were fully achieved; around one third considered that they were partially achieved; and the remaining countries indicated that the achievements could not be assessed yet.[24] However, none of the countries classified any of the intended benefits of the reforms as “not achieved.” It is an interesting contrast that, in some countries where what may be regarded as a full accrual accounting framework has already been achieved, Ministries of Finance consider that further improvements should be made.

Ministries of Finance consider enhanced accountability and increased transparency to be the main positive outcomes of the reforms. It is undeniable that accrual accounting has made more and better financial information available to the public at large. A number of countries also note that new procedures and IT systems have helped in developing the internal control environment.

Table 4. OECD countries: Achievement of reforms objectives

	Fully Achieved	Partially Achieved	Ongoing
Enhancing accountability	AUS, AUT, CAN, FIN, FRA, ISR, KOR, MEX, NZL, ESP, CHE, TUR	BEL, DNK, HUN, ISL, ITA, POL, SVK, SWE	CHL, CZE, IRL, PRT, GBR
Increasing transparency towards public at large	AUS, AUT, CAN, FIN, FRA, ISR, KOR, MEX, NZL, ESP, SVK, CHE, TUR	DNK, HUN, ISL, ITA, POL, SWE	BEL, CHL, CZE, IRL, PRT, GBR
Producing meaningful figures/financial analysts for cabinet and/or parliament and/or citizens	AUS, AUT, FRA, ISL, ISR, KOR, NZL, ESP, SVK, CHE	BEL, CAN, FIN, HUN, ITA, MEX, POL, SWE	CHL, CZE, DNK, IRL, PRT, TUR, GBR
Increasing political and public awareness about the state of public finances	AUS, CAN, FRA, ISR, KOR, MEX, NLD, NZL, SVK, ESP	AUT, CZE, FIN, ISL, ITA, POL, SWE, CHE	BEL, CHL, HUN, IRL, PRT, TUR, GBR
Better information on full costs of operations	AUS, AUT, ISL, ISR, KOR, MEX, NZL, ESP, SWE, CHE	BEL, CAN, DNK, FIN, FRA, ITA, POL	CHL, CZE, HUN, IRL, PRT, SVK, TUR, GBR
More informed decisions on asset and liability management	AUS, AUT, DNK, FRA, ISR, KOR, NZL, ESP, CHE	CAN, FIN, ISL, ITA, MEX, POL, SVK, SWE	BEL, CHL, CZE, HUN, IRL, PRT, TUR, GBR
Efficiency of the administrator's business processes	AUT, CAN, ISL, ISR, KOR, NZL, ESP	BEL, DNK, FIN, ITA, MEX, POL, SWE, CHE,	AUS, CHL, CZE, FRA, HUN, IRL, PRT, SVK, TUR, GBR

Source: OECD Accruals Survey (2016).

Satisfaction with the use of this information by external stakeholders is, however, limited. In particular:

- A number of Ministries of Finance, including early adopters of accrual accounting and/or budgeting, note that parliamentarians have limited interest in accrual financial information. This suggests that accrual financial statements remain somehow inaccessible to their primary users, and that ministries of finances still have a way to go to demonstrate their use and added value.

- Information on the full costs of operations is not always available at operational entities or units levels. Where the information is available, tools and methodologies to use it to assess and improve the management of public assets and performance of entities seem to be lacking. Some countries note also that public managers remain accountable mostly, if not only, through the appropriation process and, therefore, have limited incentive to use accrual information.

- A majority of countries also note that adoption of accrual accounting had a limited effect so far on improving the efficiency of administrative processes. This could be explained by the fact that expectations for the efficiency of internal audit and quality of accounting data increase with the adoption of accrual accounting and development of high-quality and independent audits.

The use of accrual information for macro-fiscal purpose is uneven. Most of countries that responded to the question on this issue indicated that the accrual information is not used or used only in a limited way for establishing fiscal forecasts. In many countries, the cash budget balance and net lending remain the key fiscal figures and the focus of most of the political debate. Other countries, however, in particular Australia, Austria, New Zealand and the United Kingdom, underline that efforts for harmonising the accounting basis and coverage of fiscal reports (budget, financial statements, and statistics) have allowed greater usefulness of the accounting data for fiscal analysis and greater transparency of the state of public finances.

Recent innovations are directed toward making accrual information more user-friendly and useful to budgetary decision making. Noteworthy initiatives include:

- attempts at reducing the time lapse for establishing the financial statements (for example, Austria), to make them available at an earlier stage of the budget process;
- the use of management commentaries and attempts at simplifying and streamlining the financial reports (for example, the United Kingdom) to make them more user-friendly;
- the use of accrual information to inform citizens and decision makers about the efficiency of public management (for example, New Zealand's *Investment Statement*, which measures the government's performance in managing its assets and liabilities; or the development of cross-government benchmarks for certain costs in Denmark);
- the use of technology, including the internet and business data warehousing to make information available to citizens, the parliament, and other stakeholders more easily; and
- inclusion of key ratios in notes to the financial statements to help improve understanding and financial and budgetary management.

Notes

1. Countries are classified in this category when *i)* transactions are budgeted or recognised in the financial reports at the time at which the underlying economic event occurs, regardless of when the related cash is received or paid, and *ii)* assets and liabilities are budgeted or reported in a balance sheet, irrespective of exceptions regarding the reporting or measurement method of some specific assets and liabilities.
2. Countries are classified in this category when some transactions are budgeted or recognised in the financial reports using the cash basis, and some transactions are budgeted or recognised under the accrual basis, with the final aim of adopting the accrual basis.

3. Countries are classified in this category when transactions are budgeted or recognised in the financial reports only when the associated cash is received or paid, irrespective of their reporting of commitments.

4. The management commentary, which is commonly provided in the private sector, provides readers of financial statements with a backward and forward looking analysis of an entity's financial position, financial performance, and cash flows.

5. In some jurisdictions, all employees, whether employed by the public or the private sector, are entitled to pensions from the state, which are not considered liabilities because the government can change the pension arrangements at any time.

6. For example, in Australia, social benefits do not constitute liabilities, as they are not legal obligations (not legal obligation to pay until a future point in time) and do not represent a constructive obligation (as the government does have an ability to avoid specific payments). This approach is agreed by the Auditor-General.

7 The IPSASB, however, recently published a Consultation Paper on Recognition and Measurement of Social Benefits.

8. The basic elements of an annual budget are *i)* a policy statement describing the macroeconomic assumptions on which the budget is based, presenting the fiscal objectives, targets, and the main policy decisions (new programmes or savings) of the government; *ii)* annual forecasts of revenue and expenditure, the fiscal balance, and financing need; *iii)* legal provisions to authorise or limit the incurrence of expenditure by ministry and/or programme, and to implement the policy measures adopted by the budget. In most countries of the Continental tradition, the Budget Act adopted by the Parliament combines all these basic elements. In particular, the Budget Act both forecasts and appropriates money for public policies. Countries of the Westminster tradition have a different approach and make a clear difference between forecasts and the granting of authority to spend. Fiscal forecasts are included, together with a discussion of fiscal policy and government priorities, in a budget statement that has no legal force and is normally debated in Parliament in the form of a vote of confidence (i.e., if the vote is rejected, the government must resign). Annual authority to spend is granted through Appropriation Acts (also called "Estimates") or through other laws that permanently appropriate money for specific programmes, such as entitlements.

9. They allow authorising, reporting on, and controlling future cash outflows, but are not liabilities. Some countries that use commitments in their budgets have described their budgeting system as "cash and commitment frameworks" rather than cash-basis budgeting.

10. In the survey, the category was entitled "Cash transitioning to Accruals", which did not reflect the actual situation described by most countries.

11. Within these accrual appropriations regimes, cash allocations are made available to the ministries and departments based on their estimated cash requirements, as summarised, for example, in the cash-flow statement.

12. Germany and the Netherlands use only commitment appropriations.

13. This is does not mean, though, that comparability between budget and actuals is not possible: Budget execution reports are usually comparable with the initial budget.

14. The United Kingdom highlighted its initiative, referred to as the Clear Line of Sight Project, to align estimates, budgets, and accounts.

15. In international standards, "consolidation" means presenting the assets, liabilities, net assets/equity, revenue, expenses, and/or cash flows of public sector entities as if they were a single entity. Consolidation also implies elimination of all transactions and balances between entities that are being consolidated.

16. These practices are not specifically related to accrual accounting, but are necessary and important elements of an accrual accounting framework.

17. The government's cabinet can, however, authorise deviations from IPSAS.

18. The International Monetary Fund's Government Finance Statistics Manual or the European Commission's European System of Accounts.

19. Such as the standards enacted by the INTOSAI.

20. This section of the OECD questionnaire was not completed by one respondent (United States of America).

21. See Appendix 2, Table 1.

22. See Fiscal Transparency, IMF.

23. Public information is also available for a number of European countries, and a recent study published by EUROSTAT based on a survey of EU Member States estimates that the total cost of such a reform for central government would be around 0.05% of GDP.

23. Australia and the United Kingdom are among the countries that decided to address this issue by making a strategic decision that the ministries, departments, and other agencies should absorb the costs of the reforms and that no additional funding would be provided. These included the very substantial costs of implementing new IT systems.

24. The assessment of the achievements of objectives may, however, vary depending on the stakeholders consulted.

Chapter 2

Accrual practices and reform experiences: Country profiles*

This Chapter is composed of individual country description for all 34 OECD countries. Each individual country description discusses selected accounting, budgeting, and auditing practices at the national government level; challenges associated with accrual reforms; and country's assessment of the benefits achieved.

* The statistical data for Israel are supplied by and under the responsibility of the relevant Israeli authorities. The use of such data by the OECD is without prejudice to the status of the Golan Heights, East Jerusalem and Israeli settlements in the West Bank under the terms of international law.

Australia

Preparation basis and coverage of the budget and financial reports

The budget and financial statements are prepared on an accrual basis. Both the budget and *Consolidated Financial Statements* (CFS) are composed of a full suite of statements and disclosures, as required by international standards.[1] The Government also prepares annually a management commentary. Revenue and expenditures are recorded on a full accrual basis, including losses arising from revaluation of assets and liabilities.[2] All material assets and liabilities are recorded in the balance sheet.[3] Fixed assets are measured at fair value, except for specialist defence equipment that is measured temporarily at historical cost. Tax receivables are recorded at amortised cost less impairment. Inventories are recorded at lower of cost adjusted for loss of service potential. It is to be noted that the Government accounts for social benefits on a "due and payable" basis, in accordance with international standards. This is consistent with the method of providing social benefits: They are funded from annual budget appropriations, and not as part of a formal social security scheme with premiums or contributions.

The legislature authorises expenditures on an accrual basis, with some exceptions. Appropriations are provided for all expenses projected in the accrual basis budget (operating expenditures, capital expenditures, and debt transactions), except for provisions related to asset depreciation and a number of long-term liabilities. These appropriations may be provided by a number of legal means, such as yearly appropriation legislation or special appropriations incorporated in other legislation or resulting from special account determinations.

The annual financial statements consolidate all the entities that are controlled by the Federal Government:

- The "core budget" is prepared only for the federal government (also known as the Australian Government), which is composed of ministries and their dependant bodies, offices of the House of Representatives and Senate. In addition, projections/forecasts are included in the budget documentation for public non-financial corporations and public financial corporations. The core budget is broken down further, to provide information for individual government entities. These are published as Portfolio Budget Statements;

- The annual financial statements consolidate all the entities that are controlled by the Federal Government - that is the ministries and other public bodies listed above, and the public non-financial and financial corporations. The accounting principles used by these entities have been harmonised, and their accounts are consolidated on a dedicated IT system at year-end. They also all publish their financial statements. The subnational governments (State, Territory, and Local) are independent from the central government and therefore not consolidated.

Standard setting and audit arrangements

The Australian Accounting Standards Board (AASB), an independent body, sets IFRS-based national accounting standards for the public sector. For developing the national accounting framework for the public sector, the Government has tasked the AASB with transposing IFRS, after considering their relevance in the public sector context. An important feature of the Australian public sector accounting framework is the standard AASB 1049, which harmonises accounting and statistical (Government Finance Statistics) practices. As the standards are principle-based, the MoF issues additional detailed reporting requirements and accounting guidance.

The Consolidated financial statements are audited by the SAI, in accordance with international auditing standards. The Auditor-General, an independent officer of the parliament, gives annually an opinion on whether individual financial statements of general government entities (first step of the audit) and the CFS (second step of the audit) give a true and fair view of the Government's finances. The opinion on the latest CFS reported a limitation in the scope of the audit opinion with respect to completing work on valuing specialist defence equipment at fair value, as required by a new accounting standard.

Status of accruals reform(s)

Australia completed its transition to accrual budgeting and accounting in about 10 years, as part of a broader set of reforms. Australia's transition to accrual budgeting and accounting progressed through the 1990s in conjunction with the Government's reforms for strengthening the country's fiscal position, and improving public service delivery and performance. The Ministry of Finance (MoF) was in charge of monitoring the reform and decided to implement accrual accounting progressively, by increasing over time the requirements for recording assets and liabilities.

The reform co-ordination and monitoring, and the development of the new IT systems were the main challenges during the preparation and implementation phases. A Central Task Force was set by the MoF to address the main operational tasks (designing and rolling-out the new IT system, developing guidance and manuals, and achieving a cultural change), and assist the departments. Indeed, inventories and measurement of assets and liabilities were devolved to ministries, which generated a significant work charge for them, and a need for guidance. The MoF also worked with consultants to implement some of the tasks of the transition. For example, after surveying the accounting staff skills and knowledge of accruals, the MoF developed a training strategy with a consulting firm. Lastly, the MoF tried to set realistic timeframes at each stage of the process, and worked systematically and constructively with auditors during the reform implementation.

Expected benefits, in terms of transparency, accountability, and management have been achieved. The efforts of the authorities for harmonising the accounting basis and coverage of fiscal reports (budget, CFS and monthly statistics) have allowed meeting the Government's objectives in terms of transparency, accountability, and usefulness of the data for fiscal analysis. In Australia, full accrual financial statements are included in the papers for the Budget and Budget updates; costs analysed by statistical function are presented in accrual terms; and costs of the Government's New Policy Proposals are also published in accrual terms. Asset management has also improved following the adoption of accrual accounting. The Government publishes full accrual monthly financial statements within 30 days of month end.

The budget process presents the key aggregates in both accrual and cash terms, although public attention often focuses on cash outcomes. The MoF is pursuing efforts for making the content of the financial statements more understandable to users.

Notes

1. The Australian Government also prepares a financial report entitled the Final Budget Outcome (FBO), which is released earlier than the CFS, using audit cleared data. The FBO consolidates entities by statistical sector (general government, public financial corporations, and public non-financial corporations). The FBO and all publications are prepared on an accrual basis.
2. Losses arising from revaluation of assets and liabilities are included as transactions or other economic flows, consistent with both accounting and statistical classifications
3. In Australia, natural resources are owned by the State (i.e. regional) governments and therefore not reported in the Federal Government financial statements.

Austria

Preparation basis and coverage of the budget and financial reports

The budget and financial statements are prepared on an accrual basis:

- The annual budget law is composed of an income statement that forecasts the expenses and revenues on a full accrual basis - including losses arising from revaluation of these assets and liabilities (if any), and cash flow statements. Both statements are broken down into chapters corresponding to the Government public policies set out in the Federal Organic Budget Act 2011;
- The annual financial statements are composed of a full suite of statements and disclosures.[1] Assets and liabilities are recorded in the balance sheet, except for natural resources, social benefits, and pensions, the latter being disclosed in the notes the financial statements. Assets are measured at historical cost, nominal value (tax receivables), or replacement cost (heritage assets).

Appropriations are approved on a cash and accrual basis. In Austria, the annual budget law is prepared within the cash ceiling set in the legally binding multi-year medium-term expenditure framework (MTEF).[2] The legislature approves the budget law which is composed of the income and cash flow statements mentioned above, broken down into *i) global budgets*, which set the annual amount of expenditures (accrual basis) and expenses (cash basis) for each ministry's policy area; and *ii) detail budgets*, which set out cash appropriations, expenditure and multi-year commitments levels for administrative units.[3]

The budget and financial statements cover the federal government. As required by law, the budget and financial statements cover all federal entities - that is the Federal Chancellor, ministries organised in departments, and subordinate agencies and institutions. However, only the financial statements are a consolidation *per se* of all federal entities that are considered controlled by the federal government. Federal entities follow similar charts of accounts and accounting principles for establishing their individual financial statements, which are consolidated under a dedicated IT system.

Standard setting and audit arrangements

Public sector accounting standards based on IPSASs are set out by the MoF. Standards are set in the ordinary budget law, and detailed in regulations (e.g. regulations on draft statements, valuation rules, and recognition and disclosure principles of the different elements). The draft standards are established by the MoF in co-operation with the Court of Audit, following a formal consultation process with ministries and local governments. IPSAS serve as reference standards for the national accounting standards, but some deviations exist where they are perceived as having limited impact on the steering of public finances, or generating an excessive work charge.[4]

The financial statements are audited by the SAI, in accordance with international auditing standards. The Austrian Court of Audit is an independent federal body that acts at the state, regional, and municipal levels. The Court of Audit audits annually the financial statements of federal government, and presents a report to the National Council. This report is submitted in two parts: *i)* the first part before the summer, to analyse the budget execution by chapters and inform the parliamentary debate on the MTEF; *ii)* the second and final part in autumn, to present the findings of the financial audit.[5] The most recent opinion of the Court of Audit on the financial statements was qualified due to issues with the inventory and valuation of fixed assets.

Status of accruals reform(s)

Austria completed its transition to accrual budgeting and accounting at the federal level in about 5 years, as part of a wider set of budget reforms. Due to inefficiencies of the traditional budget processes, the MoF developed reform ideas in the late 2000s with the aim to improve budgetary decision-making, and increase transparency towards the Parliament and public.[6] The MoF lobbied for political support in modernising the Federal Organic Budget Act, and managed to get approval for modifying the law in 2011. As part of these reforms, the budget and financial statements were transitioned simultaneously to the accrual basis of accounting in order to provide full information on the planned and actual costs of the ministries activities.

The reform preparation and implementation did not carry any major challenge. Thanks to studies of other countries' experiences, pilot exercises, and constant co-ordination with the Court of Audit, the MoF considers that the transition to accrual budgeting and accounting proceeded without any major difficulties. The MoF adopted a practical approach and weighted constantly expected costs vs. benefits. For example, IPSAS standards that generated an excessive work charge were not transposed into national standards as mentioned above; some assets and liabilities, as well as entities, were excluded from the opening consolidated balance sheet due to limited resources for performing inventories and valuations; and practices and tools were improved over time: regulations, guidance, and internal controls have been improved over time (and continue being improved), based on lessons learned from the first years of implementation. Another important aspect of the successful transition to accrual in Austria is the decision to rely on internal knowledge and expertise for implementing the reform: this helped monitoring the cost of transition, which is evaluated at EUR 30 million (0.007% of GDP). For IT systems, Austria chose to use corporate systems, which also prove cost-effective.

Expected benefits have been achieved, but accrual financial information is used in a limited way. The objectives of the reforms have been achieved, and accrual financial data is used at all stages of the budget process (including macroeconomic forecasts and public policies' evaluation). However, the Parliament is still making limited use of the accrual financial data. To increase the public awareness, the financial reports have been made available on the Court of Audit's website.

Notes

1. The comparison of budget and actual of the federal government is broken down by the chapters set out in the Federal Organic Budget Act 2011.
2. The MTEF contains legally binding expenditure ceilings four years in advance on a rolling basis. The ceilings apply to groups of chapters (so-called "rubrics"). Each of the five rubrics has its own expenditure ceiling, which add to one ceiling for the federal budget.
3. There are no cash appropriations for depreciation and provisions.
4. Currently Austria fully applies 20 IPSAS, partially applies 5 and does not apply 7 of 32 IPSAS.
5. Starting from 2016, there will be only one comprehensive report by the end of June. The objective is to integrate accrual information in the budget process as soon as possible.
6. The reforms package included the adoption of a binding MTEF, change of the budget structure and appropriation model; accrual budgeting and accounting; and performance budgeting.

Belgium

Preparation basis and coverage of the budget and financial reports

The federal budget is prepared on a modified cash and commitment basis. The budget bill comprises a statement that presents the federal government's current and capital expenditures (i.e., cash payments), cash receipts, financing gap, and commitments. In the budget execution outturn, expenditures are recorded as the entitlement of the third-party to payment for the delivery of goods or services is acknowledged by the administration. The legislature authorises the capital and current expenditures, commitments, and financing flows.

The year-end financial statements are prepared on an accrual basis. The annual financial statements are composed of a full suite of statements and disclosures. Tax receivables, heritage assets, civil service and military pensions, and social benefits are however not reported in the balance sheet.[1] Fixed assets reported in the balance sheet include land and buildings and infrastructure are measured at market value, and defence assets and inventories measured at historical cost.

The budget and year-end financial statements cover the federal level entities. The law defines the scope of the federal government, which is composed of *federal public services* and other federal bodies (for example, National Archives, Royal Library, Royal Museums for Art, History, etc…). Federal public services use similar charts of accounts and accounting principles, and record their financial operations in the same IT system.[2]

Standard setting and audit arrangements

The public sector accounting standards are set out by the Government and based on statistical principles. The current accounting principles have been developed with reference to Eurostat's statistics manual (the *European System of National and Regional Accounts* - ESA) and are enacted by law and royal decrees. Detailed budgeting and accounting guidance is provided in regulations prepared by the *Federal Public Service for Budget* (Budget Office). The Budget Office refers to IPSAS standards for accounting issues not dealt with by ESA.

The government's financial statements are controlled by the SAI. While financial controls over the financial operations are implemented regularly by the Belgian Court of Audit, no audit opinion has been provided yet on whether the financial statements give a true and fair view of the federal government's finances.

Status of accruals reform(s)

The federal government implements a reform for transitioning to full accrual accounting. The overall motivation for the reform, initiated by the Budget Office and Parliament, is to establish timely, transparent budgets and financial reports, covering all entities at federal government level. As part of the reform, audit procedures will be strengthened[3], and the authorities plan to develop a *Data Warehouse*, which would give direct access to the Government financial data to the Parliament.

The reform is implemented in sequenced manner, with a cautious timeline. The implementation started with federal public services in January 2009, and was progressively extended to other federal bodies. The coverage of the balance sheet is also extended progressively. The last step of the reform should be to report tax revenue on accrual basis, and consolidate all federal government bodies. The project is monitored by the Budget Office, and is expected to be finalised by January 2020. The reform implementation plan may however evolve depending on decisions made with regards to EPSAS.

Several challenges had to be overcome, both at the preparation and implementation stages:

- Bringing all stakeholders on board and harmonising practices: The Budget Office established a Commission on Public Sector Accounting comprising three working groups dedicated to *i)* accounting policies; *ii)* harmonisation of the charts of accounts; *iii)* regulations;

- Finding competencies and building knowledge: The Budget Office established a team with appropriate competencies for developing guidance and manuals, and deliver trainings; when needed, the authorities hired external consultants (for example, on issues related to the IT system);

- Performing inventories and valuations: This has been achieved progressively, with transition periods granted to federal public services;

- Delivering high quality accounting data: This was achieved by developing a new IT system and developing significantly the internal control environment (automated and manual controls).

As the reform is on-going, benefits cannot be fully assessed yet. Better financial information (in particular, cost accounting for each federal entity) and standardisation of business processes have been achieved, due mainly to the roll-out of a new IT system. The authorities noted that the integrated budget and financial reporting, using the ESA principles, allows having a more consistent set of fiscal reports for forecasting and policy decision making. However, some of the expected benefits remain to be achieved, including increasing the political and public awareness on the state of public finances, and improving assets and liabilities' management.

Notes

1. Tax receivables measured at historical cost and disclosed in the notes. Yearly payments related to pensions and social benefits are however reported in the operating statement and budget execution reports.
2. The application by the other federal bodies of similar charts of accounts and accounting principles as the Federal Public Services is foreseen as of 2017.
3. The Belgian Court of Audit should give its first opinion on the federal government's financial statements in 2020.

Canada

Preparation basis and coverage of the budget and financial reports

The federal budget and year-end financial report (the *Public Accounts of Canada*) are prepared on an accrual basis. Both documents are prepared according to similar accrual accounting standards, and composed of a full suite of financial statements and disclosures. All assets and liabilities are reported in the balance sheet, except for some intangible assets, natural resources and Crown lands that have not been purchased. Assets are measured at historical cost.

Government expenditures are authorised and reported in dedicated schedules, on a modified cash basis. The *Main Estimates* are schedules presenting the Government expenditures, by department and agency. They are required to be tabled by the President of the Treasury Board (TB) for approval by the Legislature before 31 March each year, which is usually shortly after the Budget which does not itself have a fixed tabling date. Each quarter, department and agencies report their actual spending against these estimates, and, at year-end, a comparison of estimates and actuals is included in the *Public Accounts of Canada.* In the Main Estimates, expenditures are presented on a modified cash basis of accounting: Transactions are recorded when funds are paid or are due for payment (e.g., certain goods received or services rendered prior to or on 31 March of a fiscal year, but not paid for until after that date; and write-off, forgiveness, etc… of loans, investments or advances).

The budget and financial statements present a consolidated view of public entities controlled by the federal government. In Canada, public entities include ministries, departments and agencies that report to Parliament or to Cabinet ministers, and Crown corporations. The federal budget and accounts are consolidated based on the control approach; therefore, provincial and territorial governments, which are independent of the federal government with regards to their revenue and expenditure policies, are not included. The entities that are within the scope of the federal budget and accounts follow similar charts of accounts, and accounting standards.

Standard setting and audit arrangements

The public sector accounting standards are established by an independent standard setter. Canadian federal government entities are required to comply with the accounting standards established by the Minister of Finance and the President of the Treasury Board, as stated in the federal *Financial Administration Act*. The *Public Sector Accounting Board* (PSAB), an independent standard-setter associated with the Chartered Professional Accountants of Canada, sets the accruals-based accounting standards for Canadian public sector entities (PSAS). Although IPSAS and IFRS may be used as a reference when new PSAS are developed, and these standards are based on similar conceptual frameworks, there is no current strategy for alignment with international generally accepted accounting principles. Some notable differences include more detailed guidance in some areas (for example, government transfers) and divergent approaches in others (for example, the revaluation measurement method is not permitted by Canadian Public sector accounting standards).

The Public Accounts of Canada are audited by the SAI, in accordance with international auditing standards. The Auditor General provides annually an opinion on whether financial statements present fairly, in all material respects, the financial position of the Government of Canada, and the results of its operations, changes in its net debt, and its cash flows for the year then ended in accordance with the stated accounting policies of the Government of Canada, which conform with Canadian public sector accounting standards. The Auditor General formulates observations noted during the audit of the Consolidated Financial Statements of the Government of Canada, and releases an annual update on previous observations. Recent observations were focused on improving the inventory and valuation of defence assets, the recognition and measurement of environmental liabilities, and reliability of tax revenue accounting systems and practices.

Status of accruals reform(s)

Canada completed its transition to accrual budgeting and accounting in less than 10 years. By the mid-1990s, the Parliament, Government, and MoF decided that the federal government should establish audited financial statements, on a full accrual basis, for the whole-of-government by fiscal year 2002-03. The main objective of the reform was to improve the financial information available to decision-maker, and, in particular, to evaluate the complete costs of government activities. Responsibility for implementing the reform was granted to the Treasury Board and Receiver General.

The reform preparation and implementation did not carry any major challenge. The main implementation issue was the need for new competencies and the delivery of training to existing resources. Inventories and measurement of fixed assets were carried relatively easily, thanks to early consultation and engagement between stakeholders, the development of models for costing the assets where no records existed for actual historical costs, and a manageable timeframe. New functions were developed in the IT systems in conjunction with planned updates scheduled in 2000. One explanation for this smooth reform implementation could be that changes to the Government budget and financial accounts have been sequenced, hence giving enough time to build capacities and perform lengthy operational tasks (for example, accounts payable were reported on an accrual basis at the beginning of the reform, while fixed assets were recorded at a later stage of the process).

The benefits of the reforms are acknowledged, but decision-making remains to a certain extent driven by cash considerations. Transparency and accountability are believed to have improved with the adoption of accrual budgeting and accounting, as well as the public awareness about the state of the Government of Canada's finances. Financial business processes have also been strengthened, due to sustained training and IT systems' upgrades. However, as managers in departments and agencies remain accountable only through the appropriation process, which is presented on a modified cash basis, decision-makers are believed to make limited use of accrual-based information with regards to assets and liabilities management, and evaluation of the costs of their activities.[1]

Note

1. It is noted in the Observations of the Auditor General on the *Consolidated Financial Statements of the Government of Canada for the Year Ended 31 March 2013* that, in April 2013, the government completed its study of accrual-based budgeting and appropriations, and it reported the results to the standing committees on Public Accounts and on Government Operations and Estimates. In its Report on the Assessment of Departmental Accrual Budgeting and Appropriations, the Treasury Board of Canada Secretariat concluded that it continues to support the use of accrual methods for budgeting, accounting, and reporting, but that the accounting for appropriations should remain unchanged.

Chile

Preparation basis and coverage of the budget and financial reports

The budget and year-end financial report are prepared on an accrual basis:

- The Budget Bill includes a budget statement presenting forecasts of expenses and revenue on an accrual basis. On this basis, the Legislature authorises the annual current and capital expenditures and the financing flows. Expenditures are classified into personnel expenditure, purchase of goods and services, current transfers (subdivided into all the different recipients), purchase of non-financial assets (subdivided into vehicles, machines and equipment, computer equipment and software), capital transfers (subdivided into all the different recipients), debt service and liquidity;

- The year-end financial report is composed of a balance sheet, income statement, cash flow statement, comparison of budget and actuals, and notes. Financial assets and liabilities are reported in the balance sheet, as well as some fixed assets, such as land and buildings (measured at historical cost). However, some significant elements are not reported nor disclosed so far: They include natural resources, heritage assets, infrastructure, defence assets and inventories, civil and military pensions, social benefits, and PPP debt. Revenue is reported a cash basis.

The budget covers the central government. The Chilean central government is divided into ministries and agencies, and includes the social security funds and regional governments, which are administered directly by the Government.

The year-end financial report covers the whole of the public sector, but it is not a consolidation *per se*. In Chile, the law defines the scope of the public sector. Public entities can be classified in four 'sectors': The central government (as defined above); local governments; public universities; and the state-owned enterprises. Each entity within these four categories maintains its accounts on an accrual basis. However, despite the central government and municipalities using similar charts of accounts, and public universities and SOEs applying similar accounting standards (IFRS), accounting practices are not harmonised yet. Therefore, the Government does not establish consolidated financial statements, and has chosen rather to publish a year-end financial report presenting information on the four sectors in different 'chapters'. The Budget Office of the Ministry of Finance however publishes a yearly statement of operations of the general government (central governments and municipalities).

Standard setting and audit arrangements

Accounting standards are set by the Comptroller General of the Republic (CGR). The CGR is the Governmental body in charge of the financial control on public expenditure. It also enacts the accounting standards and regulations for the central government entities and municipalities, in accordance with the broad principles set in the law.

The CGR performs regular financial controls. The CGR, in its capacity of the central government's financial control body, performs controls on the ministries and agencies' financial processes and spending, but does not give an opinion on whether the financial report is giving a true and fair view of the Government's finances.

Status of accruals reform(s)

A reform aimed at implementing IPSAS is on-going in Chile. Since 2011, central government entities have been preparing financial statements based on national accrual accounting standards. With the aim of improving public sector governance and transparency and with the support of the MoF, the CGR has decided to transpose IPSAS in the national accounting framework. This reform is monitored by the CGR and Budget Office of the MoF. The implementation of IPSAS will be sequenced: Central government entities should start implementing the new standards by 2016, while municipalities will do so at a later date.[1] In addition, a transition period of three years has been granted to central government entities for recognising certain assets and liabilities (in accordance with *IPSAS 33 First-time Adoption of Accrual Basis IPSASs*). The CGR also plans to roll-out a consolidation IT system (SICOGEN).

Standard-setting and assets' inventories are perceived as the main challenges of the preparation phase. The transposition of IPSAS in the national accounting framework was undertaken by the CGR with external assistance. Deviations from IPSAS were authorised when some accounting policies were to complex or resources intensive, and to accommodate national specificities, such as the separations between budgetary resources and those allocated to military activities. External assistance was also provided to the authorities for developing manuals and delivering training to officials, with good progress made so far. In addition, the CGR has developed IPSAS implementation guidelines, which have been sent to the entities and are implemented by most of them as of today. Inventories are lengthy operations that will be performed over the next three years by ministries and agencies, with the support of the CGR. Auxiliary IT systems will be used by public entities for recording the assets, as the existing IT systems were upgraded but not replaced.

With regards to the implementation phase, monitoring of progress made by entities is a key issue. The CGR is developing an IT system dedicated to the monitoring of IPSAS deployment in the 227 central government entities. This aims at providing adequate support to entities, depending on their observed progress.

Benefits of IPSAS implementation cannot be assessed yet. The first IPSAS based financial statements should be established in 2017. These financial statements will be published systematically, which was not mandatory prior to the reform.

Note

1. In Chile, there are 227 public entities in the Central Government, and 345 municipalities.

Czech Republic

Preparation basis and coverage of the budget and financial reports

The government's budget and budget execution reports are presented on a cash and multi-year commitment basis. The cash basis budget and year-end financial report present the government's current and capital expenditures (i.e., cash payments), cash receipts, cash balances at bank, and multi-year commitments. The legislature authorises the capital and current expenditures, financing flows, and multi-year commitments.

Accrual financial statements are also established at year-end, as supplementary information to budget execution report. The financial statements include all key statements and disclosures, and a management report comments and analyses the main figures presented in the financial statements. Assets and liabilities are reported in the balance sheet, except for natural resources, civil service and military pensions, and assets and liabilities related to PPPs. Assets are measured at historical cost, except for heritage assets that are measured at a symbolic value and assets held for sale measured at the fair value. Contingent liabilities are disclosed in the financial statements and include all material amounts they will probably result from approved contracts with third-parties.

The current coverage of the financial reports is central government, but it should be increased by the end of 2016. The Government's budget covers the central government - that is the ministries and central offices - and discloses the transfers to public agencies and non-profit institutions (such as universities and research institutions). The first consolidated financial statements will be published in 2016 and will cover the ministries and central offices, public agencies, local government entities, and SOEs.[1] The charts of accounts and standards used by these entities have been harmonised since 2010. The entities report their financial data in in a dedicated IT system managed by the MoF on a quarterly basis for statistical purposes (ESA), and at year-end for consolidation purpose.

Standard setting and audit arrangements

Accounting standards based on IPSAS are set in law and regulations. Two Acts set the framework for budgeting and accounting: The Act on Budgetary Rules enacted in 2000, and the Act on Accounting enacted in 1991. In addition, accounting regulations are enacted by the MoF for each category of public entities. The accounting standards and principles defined by the MoF are based on IPSAS, but diverge to accommodate the specificities of the public sector operations. Examples of divergences include the recognition method for taxes and measurement method for financial instruments.

The financial statements are audited by the SAI, in accordance with international auditing standards. The SAI annually undertakes the audit of the government's fiscal report and provides an opinion on whether the financial statements give a true and fair view of the Government's finances, in compliance with international auditing standards. As of today, issues with the financial statements include the general quality and consistency of the accounting data, weaknesses of internal controls, and the lack of reliability of the inventory and valuation of some assets. The audit report is presented to the Government and is also discussed with the Control committee of the House of Commons.

Status of accruals reform(s)

The authorities consider that their accrual reform is at the end of the implementation phase. The decision to adopt accrual accounting at the central government level was taken by in 2007, with the support of the Government and MoF. The motivations were mainly to improve the quality of public accounting (reliability, timeliness, etc.), and have a complete picture of the financial position of the public sector. The reform's implementation started in 2010 and will be completed in 2016.

A number of challenges had to be overcome to implement the reform. Amending the laws and regulations, establishing a reform monitoring framework, and developing adapted guidance were the main challenges with regards to the preparation of the reform. At the implementation phase, the authorities had to address issues with the IT systems and consolidation procedures, including defining the scope of consolidation.

The authorities consider that the benefits expected from the reform have been partially achieved. Improvements are still expected with respects to transparency, accountability, and management. The authorities note however that the accrual financial data is now used to establish the fiscal statistics. With regards to transparency, the authorities note that the audit report has started being published on the Government website recently.

Note

1. Public agencies are composed of so-called State extra-budgetary funds and semi-budgetary organisations. The local government is comprised of Regional Offices, Municipalities and Town Councils, Regional Councils of Cohesion, and Regions. There is no social security fund in the Czech Republic, as all social benefits are managed by the Ministry of social affairs and its subsidiary organisations.

Denmark

Preparation basis and coverage of the budget and financial reports

The budget and financial statements are prepared on an accrual basis. Both the budget and financial statements of the central government are composed of all key of statements and disclosures. Assets and liabilities are reported in the balance sheet, except for natural resources, heritage assets, civil service pensions and social benefits. Expenditures are recorded on a full accrual basis, which is not yet the case for tax revenue. Assets are measured at historical cost (the only exception is office buildings, which are measured at market value).

Appropriations mix cash and accrual elements. In Denmark, the legislature authorises the operating budget of central government entities - that is their current and capital expenditures and multi-year commitments - and the State debt. The budget and financial statements are prepared on a similar basis to allow a direct control over the compliance of financial transactions with the Parliament's authorisation. In some cases, this was made possible by choosing to record the financial transactions on a cash basis in both the budget and financial statements (for example, transfers to households). However, a full alignment was not considered feasible: A number of financial transactions are appropriated on a cash basis despite being recorded on an accrual basis in the financial statements, such as defence-related operating and capital expenditures, or capital expenditure for infrastructure.

The State budget and financial statements cover the budgetary central government. In compliance with the Constitution and law, the State budget and financial statements encompass the Government bodies, ministries, and public agencies whose operating budget is directly funded by the State. A number of central government entities remain outside of the scope of the State budget and financial statements, even when they receive a subsidy that almost fully funds their operating expenditures (that is the case, for example, with universities and secondary public schools). However, transfers and outstanding guarantees or loans between the State and these entities are reported in their individual income statements and balance sheets. State owned enterprises are not consolidated in the budget and financial statements either, but there are reported as financial asset in the State balance sheet.

Budgetary central government entities' accounting practices are fully harmonised. Budgetary central government entities practices with regards to budgeting, accounting, and financial reporting are ruled by the Constitution and Law on State Accounting. In addition, the MoF has enacted regulations for harmonising practices with regards to accounting systems and processes, such as the chart of accounts. Last, budgetary central government entities use a similar double entry bookkeeping IT system (Navision) for recording their financial transactions.

Standard setting and audit arrangements

Public sector accounting standards are enacted by the MoF. The MoF has been historically in charge of defining the accounting standards for public sector entities. Improvements to accounting standards have been done progressively, with the MoF systematically building on existing standards for refining and modernising accounting practices. Therefore, when accrual accounting was introduced for central government in 2003, the MoF, with the assistance of an Advisory Board, enacted new accounting standards that drew both on existing public sector practices and Danish private sector standards (IFRS). The MoF now considers IPSASs as references for developing or refining the accounting standards (for example, current discussions on whether the accounting treatment of civil service pensions should be aligned with the corresponding IPSAS standard).

The financial statements are audited by the SAI, in accordance with international auditing standards. The Constitution requires all public sector entities to have their financial accounts audited annually. Budgetary central government entities are audited by the Auditor General, and other central government entities are audited by "authorised" public accountants that follow audit guidelines issued by the Auditor General. All audits are conducted in accordance with international auditing standards (ISSAI). The Auditor General's opinion on the consolidated financial statements is stated in an audit report presented directly to the Parliament. The audit opinion on the latest financial statements was qualified, due to issues with the recording and measurement of overdue tax receivables and related IT systems.

Accruals implementation, challenges and benefits

Denmark has completed its transition to accrual budgeting and accounting in about five years, but improvements are made on an on-going basis. The accrual accounting reform was initiated in Denmark in 2003, following the publication by the MoF of a report entitled *Cost and Effectiveness of the State*. It aimed mainly at enhancing accountability and transparency, and having information on the full cost of the State operations. The reform was sponsored by the Government and Parliament, and monitored by the Budget Office and Treasury. Despite the reform being completed in about five years, the MoF continues working on improving the budgeting and accounting standards, and the efficiency of the financial business processes. For example, the year-end closing procedure has been shortened significantly in 2013.

The reform started after a pilot exercise, and the MoF provided significant and constant assistance and training to implementing units. The MoF ran tests in a few entities to assess the feasibility of new accounting principles and regulations. This helped in gaining the support of the Parliament for a full implementation. Based on the results of the tests, the MoF developed guidance and guidelines for assisting entities in implementing the reform and developing their internal control. A steering committee with representatives from all implementing units was also set up to share experiences and co-ordinate activities, in particular with regards to inventory and measurement of assets and liabilities. The MoF also co-ordinated with the Auditor General. Lastly, the MoF signed framework agreements with audits firms for making technical assistance available to all entities, if and when needed. In addition, both general and specific trainings were delivered to implementing units, and e-learning courses were available to staff.

The authorities consider that the expected results have been only partially achieved. During the first year of the reform, issues with accountability related to administrative costs had to be addressed. While the full cost of operations is now available, its analysis and link to performance remain limited. Meaningful figures and analysis on the cost and effectiveness of the State operations still have to be developed. To address this, the MoF has developed benchmarks for certain costs, such as salaries, and developed standardised valuation methods for overhead costs.

Estonia

Preparation basis and coverage of the budget and financial reports

The budget is prepared on a cash basis, with a transition to accrual budgeting planned for 2017. The cash basis budget presents the government's current and capital expenditures (i.e., cash payments), revenues (cash receipts), and financing transactions (transactions related to financial assets or liabilities). The legislature - the *Riigikogu* - authorises the annual capital and current expenditure and ceilings on debt and guarantees. Following pilot exercises and various preparatory tasks (including the drafting of regulations), Estonia plans to transition to accrual budgeting in 2017 (see below).

The Consolidated Annual Report of the State is prepared on a full accrual basis, and budget execution reports on a cash basis. Budget execution reports are prepared on a similar basis than the budget, to control the compliance of budget execution with the authorisation granted by the legislature. In addition, the Ministry of Finance is responsible for establishing the *Consolidated Annual Report of the State*. The financial statements are comprised of a full suite of statements, as required by international standards, and includes a management report, which describes the state's economic development, including the development of the public sector and the government sector, achievement of the goals set in the state's action plans, and performance, and gives an opinion of the state's internal control systems and the organisation of internal auditing. All assets and liabilities are recorded in the balance sheet – except for natural resources, whose value is disclosed in the notes.[1] Assets are valued at historical cost. Revenue and expenditures are recorded on a full accrual basis, including losses arising from revaluation of assets and liabilities (if any).

The *Consolidated Annual Report of the State* has a wider coverage than the budget and encompasses the whole of the public sector. The government sector is divided in four sub-sectors as follows: The State, the central government, the local government, and social security funds.[2] The budget and budget execution reports cover State entities (ministries, Government Offices, and constitutional institutions), while the Consolidated Annual Report of the State contains the following financial statements: Consolidated and unconsolidated financial statements of the state, consolidated and unconsolidated financial statements of the local governments, consolidated financial statements of the central government, and consolidated financial statements of the public sector. All public sector entities apply similar accrual basis accounting standards and charts of accounts. The consolidation is realised based on the financial data uploaded in in a web-based database.

Standard setting and audit arrangements

Accounting standards are set by the MoF. The broad principles regulating public sector accounting in Estonia are set out in the *Accounting Act* and the *General Rules for Public Sector Accounting*, which require that national standards for the public sector be established based on IPSAS. The standards are enacted by the MoF, based on the recommendations of the *Estonian Accounting Standards Board.* Detailed accounting principles and procedures are defined at entity level.

The SAI provides annually an opinion on whether the financial statements give a true and fair view of the Government's finances, in compliance with international auditing standards. The National Audit Office is responsible for auditing ministries' individual financial statements and the Consolidated Annual Report of the State. The opinion is unqualified. Public sector entities that meet the criteria set out in the *Auditors Activities Act* are audited by an independent audit firms.

Status of accruals reform(s)

Estonia completed its accrual accounting reform in two years. The transition to accrual accounting and compilation of consolidated statements was decided in 2003. The timescale for the reform was short: In 2004, accrual basis consolidated financial statements were published for the State subsector, and in 2005 the coverage was extended to the whole of the public sector. An implementation plan and capacity building and communication strategy were defined for implementing the reform.

Accrual budgeting should be implemented by 2017. The reform proposal was issued in 2008, as part of a broader reform agenda that included activity-based budgeting and an enhanced system of strategic planning and management. The implementation of accrual budgeting was expected to improve cost awareness and management control at the operational level. A pilot exercise was launched in 2010, which showed that the reform increased significantly the workload of agencies and generated resistance to the reform. In addition, the pilots showed that significant need for capacity building both at the political and operational levels. Despite these challenges, the decision to transition to accrual budgeting was taken by end of 2015, with implementation planned for 2017.

Notes

1. State's subsoil assets are estimated as the value of future fiscal revenues arising from the extraction of natural resources reserves.

2. The coverage of the subsectors is as follows: 1) State subsector - ministries and Government Office with their agencies, constitutional institutions, and government sector entities under their direct dominant influence (foundations, State Real Estate Ltd Group, Welfare Services Ltd Group); 2) Central government subsector - covers the same entities as enrolled in the state subsector and other legal persons in public law (for example besides state subsector public universities, Estonian Defence League, The Cultural Endowment of Estonia, Estonian Broadcasting, National Opera Estonia, National Library); 3) Local government subsector - all local government entities with other government sector entities under their direct dominant influence (foundations, non-profit organisations, and a few enterprises); 4) Social security subsector - Estonian Health Insurance Fund and Estonian Unemployment Insurance Fund.

Finland

Preparation basis and coverage of the budget and financial reports

The budget and budget execution report are prepared on cash transitioning to accrual basis. Depending on the expenditure item, the budget and the budget outturn are prepared either on accrual or cash basis. Additionally, the budget includes 'budget authorities' prepared on a commitment basis. The appropriations of the budget proposal are either fixed one-year appropriations, estimated appropriations, or transferable appropriations that may be carried over for two, three or five years. Spending generated by the activities of government agencies and public bodies is usually budgeted under two-year transferable appropriations, while transferable appropriations for three or five years are used to cover, for example, separately budgeted investments.[1] The legislature also authorises the debt either as financing needed for that budget year or as ceiling.

The financial statements are prepared on accrual basis, subject to a number of specific rules for non-exchange transactions and long-term liabilities. The financial statements are composed of a full suite of statements and disclosures, as required by international standards, and are published with a commentary from the Government. Transactions are reported on accrual basis, as a general rule, with a number of exceptions (for example, transfers are recorded on a due-and-payable basis and tax revenue on a cash basis). Long-term liabilities, when their value is uncertain, are not recorded in the balance but disclosed in the notes to the financial statements (for example, the civil and military pensions' actuarial value is disclosed in a note to the financial statements). Fixed assets are reported, except defence equipment, and measured at historical cost.

The budget and financial statements both cover the budgetary central government. As required by the Budget law, the budget and financial statements have a similar coverage and encompass the Presidency, the Parliament, ministries and their agencies. Other central government entities (pension and social security institutions, universities and other entities) establish individual accrual basis financial statements. Budgeting and accounting practices are fully harmonised at the budgetary central government level (see below).

Standard setting and audit arrangements

Accounting standards are set out by the Ministry of Finance (MoF), and based national private sector accounting standards. The Budget law, which dates back to 1988, and the Budget Decree, which dates back to 1992, define the broad principles applying to budgeting and accounting. The accounting standards were aligned with those applicable for the Finish private sector in 1998. Detailed accounting rules and a mandatory chart of accounts are defined in the Treasury's stipulations, instructions and accounting manual.

The National Audit Office (NAO) gives annually an opinion on whether financial statements give a true and fair view of the Government's finances, in compliance with international auditing standards. The opinion on the latest Financial Statements was qualified, due to issues with budget execution compliance, and the reliability of inventory and valuation of fixed assets.

Status of accruals reform(s)

Finland completed its transition to accrual accounting in about ten years. Finland's Government launched in 1990s a reform aiming at better evaluating performance and increasing efficiency in the public administration. In this context, accrual accounting was perceived a tool for better and more complete information on the financial performance of public entities, and increase transparency and accountability. The Treasury developed in about two years the new accounting model to be implemented by a number of pilot entities by 1997. After the pilot exercise, the legal framework was amended, and all entities were required to move to accrual accounting by 1998.

Implementation challenges were limited. The preparation work included training, changes in IT-systems, etc. The inventory of government assets and preparation of financial statements within the legal timeframe were the main challenges. To improve the timeliness of the consolidated financial statements, the Government has rolled out in 2016 a new IT system that will be used by all budgetary central government entities.

Expected benefits have been achieved partially. While transparency and accountability have been strengthened, public awareness on public finances, efficiency gains in business processes, and improvements to assets management are partially achieved.

Note

1. Investments can also be budgeted through budget authorities.

France

Preparation basis and coverage of the budget and financial reports

The Central Government's budget and budget execution report are presented on cash and multi-year commitment basis. The cash basis budget and year-end financial report present the government's current and capital expenditures on a cash and commitment basis, the cash receipts, cash balances at bank. Information on the government's stock of debt and guarantees is also included in the budget documentation.

Accrual financial statements are established at year-end. All assets, liabilities, expenses, revenues, and contingent liabilities are reported or disclosed in the financial statements. Assets and liabilities are reported in the balance sheet, except for civil service and military pensions that are disclosed in the notes to the financial statements in compliance with Central Government Accounting Standards (standard 13) and are measured using the projected unit credit method[1]. The notes to the financial statements also include a reconciliation table between the cash-based excess or deficit (provided in the budget execution report mentioned above), and accrual-based profit or loss. The measurement methods for Central Government's tangible assets are defined by class and sub-class of assets. Historical cost is the preferred measurement method, but assets may be measured using market value or replacement cost (where no other information is available, for example, infrastructure assets). Heritage assets are either measured at symbolic value or at acquisition cost. The financial statements include all primary financial statements and notes to the accounts (the Statement of changes in net assets is provided in the notes to the financial statements). A management report comments and analyses the main figures presented in the financial statements.

The budget and year-end financial report are established at the budgetary central government level. The *Central Government's Financial Report* covers the ministries, and additional public bodies fully financed by the Central Government budget (for example, the Parliament). Following a number of revisions to the legal framework (in particular, the adoption of new regulation with regards to public entities budgeting and accounting practices in 2012), all public entities prepare a budget and accrual-based financial statements, which are not consolidated.

Standard setting and audit arrangements

Accrual accounting standards are set out by an independent standard setter, and elaborated in accordance with French laws and public policies. Overall requirements applying to the budget and financial reports preparation are set in the legislative framework (Constitution, Budget Law) and in regulations. Budgeting principles are historically set by the Ministry of Finance. Accounting standards are established by an independent standard setting authority, and endorsed by the MoF. Standards are elaborated in accordance with French laws and public policies, with a foreword explaining the rationale for potential differences with the private and public sectors' international and national standards. A set of accounting standards for public entities, aligned with those applicable to the Central Government, was also recently adopted.

The Court of Account (Cour des Comptes) provides annually an opinion on whether the financial statements give a true and fair view of the Government's finances, in compliance with international auditing standards. The annual audit report is presented to the Parliament. All audit opinions on the financial statements have been qualified so far, but the number of qualifications has decreased regularly. The remaining audit qualifications are on the internal control and reliability of inventory and measurement of some specific assets. The Court of Accounts also audits the financial statements of the main Social Security entities, and audit firms are tasked with a similar mandate with regards to other public entities. Audit of local bodies' financial statements has not yet been made mandatory, but experimental audit of local government entities' financial statements will be launched in 2020 in accordance with a recent legislative requirement (cf. article 110 of the Law August 4, 2015 on new organisation of the Republic).

Status of accruals reform(s)

France completed its transition to accrual accounting in about four years. Despite the fact that some public entities implemented accrual accounting more than 50 years ago, the adoption of accrual accounting for the Central Government is perceived as the core accounting reform in France. It followed the revision of the Budget Law in 2001, which launched a wide PFM reforms agenda. Those reforms were sponsored by the Parliament, the Government (of which the MoF), and monitored by the Budget Office and an inter-ministerial task force. The first accrual financial statements were established in 2006.

A number of challenges had to be overcome to implement the reform. Developing an IT system and related guidance, delivering training, and undertaking inventories and evaluations of assets and inventories are seen as the main challenges with regards to the preparation of the reform. Efforts are now mostly focused on improving the quality of financial data, the internal control environment, and internal audit functions. As a result, since the first financial statements on accrual basis were certified (2006), eight audit qualifications have been removed (there were 13 qualifications in 2006 and 5 qualifications in 2014). Central Government accounting services are still working on removing the remaining qualifications of the Court of Audit.

Benefits associated with accrual accounting are almost fully achieved. Except for those business processes that remain to be improved in some areas, the reform delivered its expected outcomes in terms of transparency, accountability, awareness on the state of public finances, improvements to assets and liabilities management and information to stakeholders. Accrual-based data is used to establish the national accounts (statistics), albeit after a number of restatements.

Note

1. Civil service and military pensions are provided through a "repartition" mechanism and obligations that should be reflected in the financial statements exist for the reporting period only.

Germany

Preparation basis and coverage of the budget and financial reports

The German federal budget and financial report are prepared on a cash and commitment basis, with some supplementary accrual elements disclosed at year-end. The federal budget presents the payments, commitments, and receipts for the year, and a borrowing plan to cover any financial gap. The capital and operating expenditure detail is set out in departmental budgets which are approved line by line by the legislature. The *Bundestag* authorises also the ceiling on guarantees. In addition to the budget outturn, the year-end financial report includes a supplementary balance sheet, a statement of changes in net assets, and disclosures in which the cash balances at bank, provisions (including pensions), financial assets, and contingent liabilities are reported (albeit not exhaustively).

The budget and financial report cover the budgetary central government. The federal ministries and departments' expenditure and revenues are reported in the budget and year-end financial report, with chapters for each ministry, as required by the Organic Budget Law. To that purpose, the ministries and departments record their financial transactions in a centralised IT system managed by the MoF. Other federal bodies (public agencies, independent boards and commissions, as well as social security funds) are covered in the budget and financial report for the portion of their revenue transferred from the federal budget. These entities establish individual financial statements. The supplementary balance sheet discloses the value of the federal government's shares in other entities at equity value.

Standard setting and audit arrangements

Budgeting and accounting principles are set out by a dedicated administrative body. Public sector cash budgeting and accounting rules, as well as accrual accounting standards, are issued by a dedicated committee, as required by the Organic Budget Law. The members of the committee are representatives (usually from the MoF) of the federal level and the 16 states (*Länder*). It also includes participants without voting rights.[1] The rules and standards issued by the committee are enacted by the Federal and the *Länder* Governments in their respective Budget Codes and operationalised in accompanying regulations.[2]

The Supreme Audit Institution undertakes annually the audit of the year-end financial report. The Federal Court of Audit - the *Bundesrechnunghof* - controls annually the budget execution (compliance audit) and other aspects of the financial management, and presents its findings in a public audit report submitted to both the government and the parliament. The audit report is a basis for the annual parliamentary discharge procedure - that is the two Houses of Parliament individually granting discharge to the federal government for its financial operations of the year.

Status of accruals reform(s)

Accrual accounting adoption is not contemplated at the budgetary central government level, but *Länder* are authorised to implement accrual accounting. In 2010, the legal framework was amended to allow government entities, in particular Länder, to adopt accrual accounting if they so choose. Such a move, however, is not envisaged for the budgetary central government level: There is indeed little political support for such a reform, whose cost and benefit ratio is considered unlikely to be positive. Therefore, the authorities focus on further improving the cash-basis budget and financial report: Recent innovations include the inclusion of financial summaries, a functional (in contrast to institutional) orientation of the ministries' budget plans, and program budgeting (for instance on transport, social security or subsidies).

Notes

1. Federal Court of Audit, Federal Statistical Office, Central Statistical Agency of the State Finance Ministers, and a representative of the State Ministries of the Interior, which are responsible for setting local government accounting standards

2. Changes in the Federal Budget Code are subject to an ordinary legislative procedure, administrative regulations are changed by a uniform decision of the federal government.

Greece

Preparation basis and coverage of the budget and financial reports

The State budget and budget execution report are presented on a cash and commitment basis. The cash basis budget and year-end budget execution report include the government's current and capital expenditures (i.e., cash payments), cash receipts, debt, and commitments.[1] The Legislature authorises the current and capital expenses, debt, and commitments. The budget also includes provisions for appropriations for debt amortisation payments and interest payments on a cash basis.

Financial statements are established on cash transitioning to accrual basis. The financial statements include all key statements and disclosures, except for the Statement of changes in net assets. However, these statements are incomplete as the transition to accrual accounting is still in a very early stage: Only accrued expenses and revenue (and related assets and liabilities: Payables and tax receivables), debt, and guarantees are reported or disclosed in the financial statements so far. Tax receivables are measured at historical cost.

The budget and year-end financial report cover the budgetary central government (the "State"). The State financial report covers the Hellenic Parliament, Presidency, independent authorities, ministries and their regional agencies, and decentralised administrations. None of these entities are preparing individual financial statements, and the State accounts are maintained as those of a single entity by the General Accounting Office in the MoF, in a dedicated IT system.

Standard setting and audit arrangements

Accounting standards are established by the MoF. Requirements applying to the budget and financial reports preparation are set in the legal framework. Within this legal framework, accounting standards are established by the MoF, in consultation with an advisory board. As the accounting basis is currently in between cash and accrual, IPSAS and IFRS are not considered as a reference.

The government's financial reports are audited by the SAI. The Court of Audit provides annually an opinion on whether financial statements give a true and fair view of the Government's finances, in compliance with international auditing standards. The latest audit opinion was qualified, on the grounds that the financial statements are not prepared on a full accrual basis yet.

Status of accruals reform(s)

The MOF is planning a transition to accrual accounting at State level. The MoF is currently planning a transition to accrual accounting for State entities and is working on harmonising accounting systems and practices (chart of accounts, accounting standards, etc.). As a first step, a working group has been established by MoF - General Accounting Office with the task to create a common Chart of Accounts and accounting standards based on international frameworks (GFSM, ESA, IPSAS), until the end of September of 2016. Participants In the working group are staff from General Accounting Office, members of the advisory board, a professor of the Economic University and a member of the Court of Audit.

Note

1. In Greece, commitments are appropriations for repaying arrears due to third parties.

Hungary

Preparation basis and coverage of the budget and financial reports

The government's budget and budget execution reports to the Parliament are presented on a commitment and cash basis. The budget and year-end budget execution report present the government's current and capital expenditures (i.e., cash payments), cash receipts, cash balances at treasury/bank, debt, commitments, and guarantees. In accordance with the *Act on Public Finance*, the budget is composed of an overall budget statement and chapters presenting separately the revenues and expenditures of each budgetary units, tax revenues, transfers to local governments, and public debt service. The legislature authorises all expenditures - i.e., the capital and current expenditures, transfers, and public debt service. Budget execution reports present information on appropriations used, expenditures, commitments, and outstanding payment obligations.

Accrual financial statements are established annually. At year-end, accrual financial statements are prepared to complement the budget execution reports. They include all key statements and disclosures, except for the statement of changes in net assets. Assets and liabilities are reported in the balance sheet, except for natural resources, heritage assets, and provisions (incl. social benefits). Assets are evaluated at historical cost, with other measurement methods authorised in specific cases. Revenue and expenditures are recorded on an accrual basis, albeit with a number of exceptions.

The budget and budget execution reports to the Parliament cover the central government as defined in the legislation. Detailed budgets (or chapters) are prepared for the ministries, budgetary units, budgetary funds, and the social security funds. Despite local governments' budgets not being included in the annual budget bill, estimations of their annual expenses and revenues are presented for information to the Parliament with the Budget bill.

The financial statements aggregate the central and local government's financial statements. In compliance with accounting regulations, consolidated financial statements should be prepared by the Hungarian State Treasury. However, significant differences in entities' accounting data presentation, issues with quality of the financial data, and discrepancies in intra-group flows have not allowed so far realising this consolidation. At this stage, only the central government and local government entities' balance sheets are therefore aggregated for presentation to the Parliament.

Standard setting and audit arrangements

Central and local government entities of the full budgetary sector follow the same budgeting and accounting principles enacted by the Government. A Government Decree dating from 2013 and effective from 2014 sets out the principles applying to budgeting (cash basis), and accounting (accrual basis), and defines budgetary entities' reporting obligations (presentation, content, closing dates, etc…). The rules and principles enacted by the Government do not follow systematically the principles set out in international standards (for example, provisions are not reported in the balance sheet). While, according to the law, budgeting and accounting standards are set out by the

Government, an advisory role has been granted to the State Audit Office and administrative bodies in charge of fiscal statistics.

The SAI undertakes compliance audits on budget execution. The Hungarian State Audit Office (SAO), which follows the international professional rules of auditing enacted by INTOSAI, undertakes compliance audits annually. The findings and conclusions of these audits are presented in a public reports. As of today, findings include concerns over the general quality and consistency of the accounting data, weaknesses of internal controls, and the lack of reliability of the inventory and valuation of some assets. Due to its limited resources, the SAO has started undertaking financial audits on a limited number of Government entities.

Status of accruals reform(s)

The authorities consider that their accounting reform is completed, but they continue improving the quality and timeliness of the accounts. The decision to establish accrual financial statements in addition to the traditional cash accounts was taken in 2013 by the Government. The main motivations for the reform were to improve the quality of public accounting and the transparency and accountability. The reform was monitored by the *Government Regulation and Accounting Department* and Treasury and implemented in less than one and a half year.

The main challenges consisted in amending the existing regulations, upgrading the IT systems, and building capacities. The IT systems were modified and updated within the existing maintenance contracts. The draft regulations and instructions were discussed with several public sector accountants before being enacted, and a large training programme was delivered. Despite the preparation, some delays were experienced for establishing the first accrual financial statements in 2014. Challenges remain though, as staff capacities need to be significantly strengthened. To address this issue, the MoF is preparing more detailed accounting guidance, tries improving the quality controls on the accounting data, and develops the internal audit function. Treasury resources were strengthened for realising checks and verifications on the accounting data.

The reform's objectives have not yet been achieved. With regards to transparency, accountability, and financial analysis, initial objectives have been partially met. The authorities note however that the accrual financial data is now used to establish the fiscal statistics, and that the information on the stocks of payables and receivables is used for preparing the budget. The quality, timeliness and completeness of the accounting data need to improve for fully meeting the objectives of the reform, including the publication of consolidated financial statements. There are no plans to move to accrual budgeting as the current system of commitment appropriations backed by a cash envelope is considered as best suited to budgetary oversight and control.

Iceland

Overview of budget and financial reports

The budget and year-end financial statements are prepared on an accrual basis, subject to a number of modifications. Both the budget and financial statements are composed of all key statements and disclosures, as required by international standards, except for the statement of changes in net assets. Financial liabilities, financial assets, and provisions are reported in the balance sheet, except for social benefits, PPP liabilities, and derivatives. Investments are reported as expenditures instead of being recognised as assets and depreciated on their useful life.

The legislature authorises expenditures on a commitment and cash basis, and budget execution reports are prepared accordingly. The legislature authorises the current and capital expenditures, debt, and commitments. In the budget execution reports, expenditures are recorded based on payments (transfers, interests, and tax revenue), and commitments or invoices (operating and capital expenditures).

The budget and financial statements will present a consolidated view of public sector in the future. According the new Organic Budget Law adopted by the Parliament in 2015, the budget and financial statements should consolidate all entities controlled by the State - that is the ministries, public agencies, social security funds, and State-owned enterprises (SOEs). The authorities have been preparing for the implementation of the new law during the last few years, and plan to expand the coverage of the fiscal reports in a phased manner over the next years.

Standard setting and audit arrangements

National standards will be progressively replaced by IPSASs. Accounting standards for the public sector have been historically set by the MoF, in consultation with an Advisory Board. The national public sector accounting standards are based on those applicable for the private sector, with deviations where needed. The new Organic Budget Law has however adopted IPSAS as the reference framework.

The Icelandic National Audit Office (NAO) has a legal mandate for giving annually an opinion on whether financial statements give a true and fair view of the Government's finances, in compliance with international auditing standards. The financial audits performed by the NAO covers about 250 institutions and enterprises that are completely or primarily financed by the state and around 100 other budgetary items. The opinion is included in the year-end financial statements. The latest opinion was qualified due to issues with the general consistency and quality of the accounting data.

Status of accruals reform(s)

Iceland's accrual reform has been implemented progressively, with the final step towards full accrual accounting and budgeting planned over the next years. Accrual accounting and budgeting were introduced in 1998 in Iceland, albeit in a modified form.

The recent adoption of a new Organic Budget Law, which introduces a longer-term approach to fiscal policy-making in Iceland, has launched a new wake of reforms in the accounting and budgeting area: *i)* the budget and financial reports will cover the whole public sector, and *ii)* IPSAS become the reference framework for public sector accounting at the State level. This will lead to major changes in budgeting and accounting practices, and financial information available to the public.

The authorities are preparing for the reform implementation, with fixed assets inventory and valuation and consolidation seen as the most challenging tasks. The reform implementation will be monitored by the Treasury, an inter-ministerial team, and a number of agencies (in particular the *Government Financial Management Authority*). The preparatory tasks include: Defining the needs with regards to IT systems, developing guidance and manuals, and monitoring training delivery. The authorities expect that fixed assets inventory and valuation and consolidation of the whole of the public sector will take a few years to implement.

The full benefits of the reform cannot be assessed yet. As noted above, reforms are on-going and the full benefits of accruals implementation are still to be assessed. However, since 1998, Iceland produces forecasts on accrual basis for revenues and expenditures (for example, pensions and interests are accrued) and accrual-based fiscal ratios have started being used for analysing the impact of fiscal policies.

Ireland

Preparation basis and coverage of the budget and financial reports

The budget and year-end financial reports for central Government Departments and Offices are prepared on a cash basis, and include supplementary accrual information:

- The budget presents the Government expenses (cash payments), tax revenues (cash receipts), and financing gap. In addition, for each department of the Government, expenditures schedules (Estimates) are presented to the Legislature - the *Dáil Éireann* - for approval;[1]

- The year-end financial report (Appropriation Account) is comprised of a cash based outturn, as well as supplementary information on multi-year commitments on investment projects, cash balances at bank, debt and financial instruments, some fixed assets, and contingent liabilities including guarantees.

- In addition, to the statutory requirements, the Appropriation Account of a Government Department or Office incorporate further information of an accruals nature in the notes to the accounts including a partial balance sheet and operating cost statement.

The budget and year-end financial reports cover the central government:

- Budgetary forecasts cover the Central Government. However, the Budget includes fiscal projections for General Government revenue and expenditure prepared in line with the European Statistical Standard ESA 2010. This additional reporting results in the Budget including the revenue and expenditure of Central Government, but also the revenue and expenditure of other sectors such as Local Government and extra-budgetary funds such as the Social Insurance Fund. Estimates of revenue and expenditure of all sectors of general government are also published on a monthly basis;

- Only the cash operations processed through the Central Fund operated by the Ministry of Finance are presented in the Finance Accounts. The Exchequer Account of the Central Fund is used for recording the cash issues to central Government Department and Offices, and a number of independent entities (e.g., Parliament), With regards to extra-budgetary central Government entities (incl. the Social Insurance Fund) and Local Government, only the grants received from the Exchequer are reported.

Standard setting and audit arrangements

Budgeting and accounting principles are set out in the law and regulations. The principles of Government accounting are mainly derived from the Constitution, and from the institutional and financial relationships between parliament and the executive which have been developed over the years. The current cash basis system is set out in legislation, in particular the Exchequer and Audit Departments Act of 1866. Accounting rules for Government Departments and Offices are set out in a Public Financial Procedures manual and relevant Government Accounting Circulars issued periodically by the *Department of Public Expenditure and Reform* (DPER).

A compliance audit is undertaken annually by the SAI. As required by the Irish Constitution and statute law, the *Comptroller and Auditor General* (C&AG) performs annually a compliance audit with regard to the use of public resources, and reports its findings to the Parliament.[2] The C&AG also confirms in his report that the Appropriation Accounts have been prepared in the form prescribed by the Minister for Public Expenditure and Reform (MPER), and in accordance with standard accounting policies and principles for Appropriation Accounts.

Status of accruals reform(s)

An accrual reform is under consideration. The DPER is currently examining the feasibility of a move to accrual accounting for central Government Departments and Offices, taking account of the wider reform agenda, in particular the roll-out of the Financial Management Shared Services (FMSS), developments at EU level concerning the future implementation of harmonised accounting standards (EPSAS), and recommendations of the International Monetary Fund (IMF).[3] The move to accrual accounting for central Government Departments and Offices will also be progressed in line with developments on the FMSS and EPSAS projects. The DPER expects that the main challenges will relate to adapting the existing law and regulations; setting appropriate accounting standards; developing the necessary IT systems; and performing inventories of assets and liabilities. A working group has been established to consider the issues involved in a transition from cash to accrual accounting for central Government Departments and Offices. The Group is considering a pilot project to determine the degree to which existing reporting structures can be used to report on an accruals basis, and to consider what financial statements should be developed for reporting on an accrual accounting basis. The working group will also draw on the experiences of other EU countries in their transition from cash to accrual accounting.

Notes

1. Debt financing is handled by standing legislation rather than annual appropriation.
2. The main statutory functions of the Comptroller and Auditor General are 1) to ensure that no money is issued from the Central Fund held by the Minister for Finance except for purposes approved by the Parliament; and 2) to audit Government accounts for accuracy and regularity, and to carry out such examinations as he or she considers appropriate in regard to economy and efficiency on the use of resources and the effectiveness of certain management systems (i.e. a Value-for- Money Audit).
3. See Ireland Fiscal Transparency Assessment.

Israel

Preparation basis and coverage of the budget and financial reports

The central government's budget is established on a cash basis. The budget is composed of four main schedules (State revenues, State expenditures, earmarked revenues, and revenues and outlays of state enterprises), which are divided into parts (for example, State expenditures are divided in 3 parts: ordinary expenditures - incl. investments, transfers, and outlays). Revenues and expenditures are presented on a cash basis. The legislature, the *Knesset*, authorises the State expenditures, which are detailed in sections, subsections, and items.

The year-end financial statements are prepared on an accrual basis. The financial statements are composed of the key statements and disclosures required by international standards, except for the cash flow statement. The financial statements include specific disclosures on PPPs, guarantees, and extra-budgetary funds. All assets and liabilities, including civil service pensions, are reported in the balance sheet, except for natural resources and heritage assets. The preferred measurement method for assets is historical cost. With regards to budget execution, the financial statements include a statement on income and expenditure containing all schedules and part of the initial budget.

The financial statements provide an aggregated view of the public sector. The coverage of the financial statements has been increased progressively, and includes now all the entities controlled by the State, including state owned enterprises (SOEs). However, the non-commercial and commercial entities do not follow the same accounting standards and some entities that are still operating on cash basis. Therefore, the financial statements are prepared at year-end under a dedicated IT system using reporting packages that may in some cases be incomplete, and include estimates where needed.

Standard setting and audit arrangements

National standards based on IPSAS are developed by an independent standard setting board. In 2004, under the impulsion of the Accountant General, a resolution N°2375 was adopted that required the adoption and implementation the IPSASs for all ministries and non-commercial statutory corporations.

The consolidated financial statements are controlled annually by the SAI. The State Comptroller (SC) an independent governmental body that reports exclusively to the legislature. The SC performs regular controls on budget operations and financial management, and provides recommendations to the Accountant General, but does not deliver an opinion on the consolidated financial statements.[1] However, the Accountant General has started over the last years appointing independent auditors for performing financial audits of ministries and public agencies' financial statements.

Status of accruals reform(s)

Israel has completed its transition to accrual accounting for the public sector in about ten years. The reform started in the mid-2000s and aimed at providing the general public, decision makers, and other users with transparent, reliable and comprehensive financial information. The reform was implemented in a sequenced manner, the most recent and last step being the publication of the consolidated financial statements of the Government of Israel in 2013. The authorities consider that all the benefits expected from the reform have already been achieved. Efforts continue, though, as the coverage of the financial statements and quality of the financial data are constantly improved.

Implementing accrual accounting generated significant challenges in almost all areas. This is due to the fact that public entities had to transition from pure cash accounting to a demanding accrual system, and accommodate the demanding requirements of the consolidation process. To address these challenges, the Accountant General chose to implement accrual accounting in a gradual way, which gave sufficient time to handle the difficult task of harmonizing of accounting practices, rolling-out a centralized IT system (*Merkava*), and delivering an ambitious training and mentoring programme for public accountants and other civil servants.

Note

1. The State Comptroller Law defines the duties and areas of investigations of the State Comptroller, which include control of legality, efficiency, and preservation of Government property.

Italy

Preparation basis and coverage of the budget and financial reports

The budget and financial report are prepared on a cash and commitments basis. On the expenditure side, the budget presents the current and capital expenditures (legal commitments and cash payments), and financial obligations under multi-annual projects (multi-year commitments). It also includes information on the government's cash balances. Expenditure arrears - that is arrears related to debt repayments, suppliers or social benefits - and some government's assets are reported as memorandum items. The legislature authorises the capital and current expenditures, commitments, and borrowing. The year-end financial report's is comprised only of a statement of comparison of budget and actuals, and a set of notes and disclosures. Supplementary financial statements (*Conto del patrimonio)* are also prepared, which disclose the value of some government's assets and liabilities, such as financial debt. However, these assets and liabilities are not reported exhaustively (for example, civil and military service pensions are not measured).

The budget covers the ministries only, but a supplementary consolidated budget for the General Government is also disclosed. The government's budget coverage is limited to ministries, consistent with the legal requirements, with transfers to local governments and public agencies are reported as expenditures. In addition, an appendix to the *Stability Law* provides a consolidated general government budget statement, which covers the ministries, State agencies, constitutional and other public bodies, social security funds[1], and the local government.

The year-end financial report has a wider scope than the budget. The year-end financial report's scope is defined by law. The list of government's entities includes the ministries, State agencies, constitutional and other public bodies, social security funds, and the local government. The charts of accounts and standards used by government's entities have not been harmonised yet. For consolidation purpose, the entities restate their financial operations in a dedicated IT system.

Standard setting and audit arrangements

Accounting standards are enacted by the MoF. Broad accounting rules are defined in the law, and detailed cash accounting policies are detailed by the MoF in regulations and circulars. However, due to past attempts at transitioning to accrual accounting, some accounting rules have been defined for recording and measurement accrual elements such as fixed assets, inventories, and tax receivables. They prescribe that these assets be measured at historical cost.

The SAI undertakes annually a compliance audit of the government's financial report. This consists in verifying comprehensively the application of the applicable laws, regulations, and circulars with regards to public spending and recording of the government's financial operations. The latest report published by the SAI formulates a number of comments on the government's financial report.

Status of accruals reform(s)

A reform aiming at harmonising public entities' accounting frameworks and adopting accrual accounting was decided in 2009. The Government, with the Parliament's approval, adopted a law that sets broad reforms' objectives with regards to public accounting modernisation. According to this law, public entities, at central and local levels, should use similar accounting standards principles and charts of accounts, and adopt accrual accounting as complementary information to mandatory cash-based budget execution reports.

The objectives set out back in 2009 have not been achieved yet. The Budget Office is in charge of monitoring and implementing the reform, and has set up a working group with a mandate for modernising public accounting standards and practices. Progress in implementing the reform has been limited so far, mainly because of the complexity of the public administration rules and organisation, and Constitutional constraints. However, a cultural shift in the Government towards accrual accounting is noticeable, and accrual basis financial statements have started being established by some public entities, even if not on a regular basis.

In this context, benefits and outcomes of accrual accounting remain to be assessed in Italy. One of the main reform's expected outcomes is to bring Italy's public accounting in line with the principles set by the EU Directive 85/2011[2]. Another desired benefit is to strengthen the evaluation of the general government's financial situation and performance in economic terms.

Notes

1. The main Social Security Body is the INPS, to which retirement payments are remitted for public and private sector employees and also self-employed workers. In addition to INPS, 16 funds delivering social security services for liberal profession (doctors, accountants, lawyers, engineers, etc.).

2. Chapter II, article 1 : "As concerns national systems of public accounting, Member States shall have in place public accounting systems comprehensively and consistently covering all sub-sectors of general government and containing the information needed to generate accrual data with a view to preparing data based on the ESA 95 standard. Those public accounting systems shall be subject to internal control and independent audits."

Japan

Preparation basis and coverage of the budget and financial reports

The *General Account Budget* is established on a cash basis.[1] On the expenditure side, the budget presents the government's budgeted current and capital expenditures (i.e., cash payments). It also includes information on the government's cash balances, and the debt and guarantees' stock. The legislature authorises capital and current expenditure and borrowing.

A cash basis budget outturn and supplementary financial statements are established at year end. The authorities consider that two sets of reports serve different purposes:

- Budgetary accounting on a cash basis is mandatory: It insures comparability with the government budget, which is also prepared on a cash basis; it is also relatively simple and easy to understand by stakeholders; last, it is more "objective" than accrual accounting;

- Accounting on an accrual basis is supplementary: It captures a broader range of economic operations and thus allows evaluating government's services at full cost; it also allows having an evaluation of the government's financial position and its changes over time. The financial statements are comprised of all key statement and disclosures. Assets and liabilities are reported in the balance sheet, except for natural resources, heritage assets, and civil and military service pensions. Tax receivables are accounted for on a semi-accrual basis.[2] Measurement methods for assets vary: Land and buildings are measured at market value, and infrastructure and military assets at historical cost.

The consolidated financial reports are established at the central government's level. The government's financial reports cover the ministries, Special Accounts[3], and public agencies under the government's control. These agencies are in charge of implementing public policies, based on directions and objectives set by the ministries. The public entities establish stand-alone financial statements. The charts of accounts and standards used for doing so have not been harmonized at all levels of the central government yet. Therefore, for consolidation purpose, the entities establish a consolidation package at year-end, which is sent to the MoF. These packages are consolidated manually (Excel).

Standard setting and audit arrangements

The accounting standards are enacted by the Fiscal System Council (FSC), an advisory body for the MoF. The public sector standards are based on the Japanese accounting standards for the private sector. While there is no legal constraint for aligning the national public sector accounting standards with international frameworks (IFRS or IPSAS), the FSC has engaged, over the last years, in this exercise. The authorities highlighted in particular one difference between generally accepted accounting principles and the Japanese accounting standards for the public sector: It is that cash payments and receipts may still be recorded after the end of the fiscal year, during a "complementary accounting period".

The SAI audits annually the government's financial report. The government's financial reports, which consolidated the General Account and Special Accounts, are prepared based on accounts audited by *Board of Audit of Japan,* an organisation independent from the Cabinet and the legislature according to article 90 of the Constitution of Japan. Special accounts financial reports in government's financial reports are audited in accordance with a specific legislation, the *Act on Special Accounts*. The financial reports are reviewed by the Fiscal System Council, located within the MoF, before they are published.

Status of accruals reform(s)

Japan completed its transition to accrual accounting at the core government level in five years. The reform was initiated by the FSC and implemented by the Public Accounting Office (PAO) established in the Budget Bureau. The transition to accrual accounting was launched in 2000, when the authorities started publishing the opening balance sheet which consolidated the General Account and Special Accounts. The consolidated financial statements including public agencies started to be published in 2005.

The reform preparation and implementation did not carry any significant challenge. The PAO monitored the reform implementation. Assets and liabilities were measured based on principles established by the FSC, taking into accounts the national specificities and constraints. The full suite of accounting standards applicable to ministries was enacted in 2004 only.

The evaluation of the full cost of public policies is the main outcome of the reform. In Japan, there are 142 *Policy Units* within the government (from 5 to 15 by ministry in 2014), each one of them being in charge to implement a given public policy. Each ministry prepares the *Policy Unit Cost Statements*, which report the operating costs of each policy unit on an accrual basis. These statements are established to facilitate the evaluation of the public policies' implementation costs, and allocate resources to Policy Units in a more transparent and efficient way. However, the expected benefits in terms of transparency and accountability are partially achieved. Interest in accrual basis financial statements remains limited so far. To address this issue, the MoF decided recently to publish brochures presenting with non-technical terms the content of the financial reports.

Notes

1. The General Account Budget is the account to finance the government's major public programmes implemented by the ministries, such as social security, transfers to local government, public works, defence, or education.
2. Japan records only tax receivables that are uncollected tax assessments.
3. Special Accounts Budgets are established by legislation. Some of them have their distinct source of revenue.

Korea

Overview of financial reports

The central government's budget is established on cash basis. In Korea, the central government's budget consists of a general account and around 80 special accounts and funds.[1] In the annual budget, the core statements are the tables of total and net revenues and expenditures presented on cash basis. Supplementary information is provided, such as an evaluation of future Treasury financial obligations (commitments), and the estimated balance sheet and income statement of the funds. The legislature authorises the current and capital expenditures, commitments, financing flows, and the debt ceiling (ceilings on State bonds and loan funds borrowed).

The central government's financial statements are established on accrual basis. At year-end, a *Statement of accounts* is prepared, which is composed of the budget outturn, financial statements, and performance reports. The financial statements comprised the *financial condition statement* (i.e., balance sheet*), financial operation statement* (i.e., income statement), statement of changes in net asset, and notes. The balance sheet is relatively comprehensive and includes civil service pensions, but some elements are not reported, which include natural resources, heritage assets, defence assets and inventories, and social benefits. Fixed assets and tax receivables are measured at market value.

The budget and financial statements both cover the central government. The National Finance Act sets the broad budgeting and accounting principles. The Act requires the budget and Statement of Accounts to cover the central government accounts and funds, which are managed by the Treasury and various public entities. To this purpose, government agencies and fund-managing entities annually submit a statement of accounts to the MoF, prepared with similar accounting standards and principles. The Treasury combines these statements to prepare the *Statement of accounts*.

Standard setting and audit arrangements

The Ministry of Strategy and Finance (MOSF) of Korea establishes the national accounting standards. The *National Finance Act* sets out broad budgeting and accounting principles. The public sector standards are enacted by the MOSF, after receiving advice from the *National Accounting System Deliberation Committee* (NASDC) and the *National Accounting Standards Center* (NASC), which conducts research on local and international standards. The national public sector standards are based on IPSAS, but some deviations occur.

The financial statements are controlled by the SAI. The Statement of accounts is controlled by the *Board of Audit and Inspection*, and reviewed by the Cabinet, before being submitted to the National Assembly.

Status of accruals reform(s)

The central government has completed its transition to accrual accounting in 2 years only. In 2009, following a proposal by the MoF, the accrual basis of accounting and double-entry bookkeeping, were adopted for the central government, with the support of the Parliament. The objective was to increase transparency, and enhance the credibility of the Government finances. All accounting central government entities were required to prepare accrual basis financial statements by 2011, with the support of the Budget office.

The authorities consider that there were no major challenges with regards to the preparation and implementation of the reform. The reform implementation was relatively easy as the authorities had already rolled out a new integrated IT system (d-Brain System) in 2007, which manages all budget operations for the central government (budgeting, budget execution, settlement of accounts and performance management).

The authorities consider that all benefits expected from the reform have been achieved. The benefits achieved after the reform include better information and understanding of the state of public finance, the possibility to develop performance-based fiscal management through the calculation of full costs by project, and transparency of financial information through standardised financial statements. This has led to a better financial management too, as liabilities, including pensions, are now monitored. To increase the transparency on public finances, the MoF has adopted an open data policy: All fiscal data, Statements of Accounts and individual financial statements, are available on the MoF website.

Note

1. The budget of the central government consisted of 1 general account, 18 special accounts, and 64 funds. General account revenues are comprised of taxes and non-tax revenues - such as proceeds from the sale of shares of state-owned enterprises. General account expenditures are used to implement public policies (defence, education, etc.). Special accounts are different from the general account, established to raise revenue for a specific project or other designated purposes. Special account revenues can only be spent on the designated areas determined by each applicable act. Funds, established according to provisions of legislations, are flexibly used for specific purposes and are operated independently of the budget.

Luxembourg

Preparation basis and coverage of the budget and financial reports

The government's budget and financial report are established on a modified cash basis. The cash basis budget presents the government's expenditures and revenue, the stock of debt and guarantees, and multi-year commitments. The government's financial report presents only the government's expenditures and revenue and cash balances at bank. The legislature authorises the expenditure and debt.

Accounting principles for recording expenses and revenue differ. Expenditures and non-tax revenues are authorised and recorded on a commitment basis.[1] With regards to cut-off, commitments can be paid until the 30 April of the year following the budget year (commitment not paid by that date have to be authorized and recorded in the next budget year). Tax revenues and financial transactions are authorised and recorded on a cash basis. However, estimations of future tax revenue for a four-year period are presented in the multiannual budget.

The budget and financial report are established with a different coverage. The Government's budget covers the Head of State (Grand Duc), Government bodies, ministries and entities operating under their auspices, and Specials Funds. With regards to public agencies, the local government, social security fund, and SOEs, only transfers are disclosed in the budget. The financial report covers only the ministries and entities operating under their auspices. The other public entities establish individual financial statements.

Standard setting and audit arrangements

Accounting standards are set out by the MoF. Central government entities (with a few exceptions) follow similar budgeting and accounting principles set by law. Detailed guidance and requirements is provided in regulations and circulars enacted by the MoF.

The government's financial reports are reviewed by the Supreme Audit Institution (SAI). The SAI reviews the internal control systems and performs compliance controls on a sample of revenue and expenditure operations. No report is published following these controls. In addition the SAI publishes a report about the annual fiscal report.

Status of accruals reform(s)

The government plans to adopt accrual budgeting and accounting. The authorities are planning to adopt accrual budgeting and accounting, the reference framework being the future EPSAS. The preparation for this reform started with assessing the capacities of the IT system, but the authorities anticipate that the main challenge will be to train officials from the budget department and public accountants to new concepts and procedures. Another concern is the inventory and valuation of assets, which has not started yet.

Note

1. Articles 8 and 9 of the Budget Code

Mexico

Preparation basis and coverage of the budget and financial reports

The budget and year-end financial report are prepared on accrual, cash, and commitment basis. The budget consists of a balance sheet, an operating statement, and a budget statement. Fixed assets such as land and buildings, infrastructure and defence assets, financial assets and liabilities are reported in the balance sheet. Natural resources, heritage assets, civil and military pensions, social benefits, as well as PPP debt are not measured yet. Tax receivables (incl. tax claims of the administrations disputed by taxpayers) are only disclosed as a memorandum item. The income statement and budget statement present the Government's expenditure and revenue, on an accrual, cash, and commitment basis. The Legislature approves budget statement - i.e., the commitments, cash payments, and taxes collection.[1] In addition, the legislature authorises the debt ceiling.

The budget and financial statements do not have a similar coverage. The budget covers the ministries, other Government bodies (legislative, and judiciary, branches), and public enterprises.[2] Transfers to other public entities are recorded as expenditure. Since 2015, the annual financial statements cover, in addition to the above, the autonomous entities and the parastatal sector. The entities consolidated are those that are under the control of the federal Government. Similar charts of accounts and accounting standards are used for preparing individual financial statements, which are consolidated automatically, under a dedicated IT system.[3]

Standard setting and audit arrangements

Accounting standards are set out by an independent standard-setter. Broad principles applying to budget and accounts' preparation and presentation are set by law. Accounting standards are defined by the National Council of Accounting Harmonisation (*Consejo Nacional de Armonización Contable*, CONAC), an independent standard setter.

The year-end individual and consolidated financial report are audited by the SAI, in accordance with the applicable international audit standards. The *Auditorìa Superior de la Federacìon* (ASF) audits the consolidated year-end financial report and the individual accounts of all public entities, except public corporations, which are audited by audit firms. The ASF provides an opinion on whether the financial reports give a true and fair view. With regards to the consolidated financial statements, issues with the consolidation scope and the quality and consistency of the underlying accounting data have been mentioned in recent audit reports.

Status of accruals reform(s)

Mexico completed its transition to accrual accounting in 2015. The General Law of Government Accounting (*Ley General de Contabilidad Gubernamental*) was adopted in 2008, with the sponsor of the Parliament, Government, and MoF. According to this law, public entities, at the federal, regional (States), and local (municipalities) levels, should use similar accounting standards principles and charts of accounts, and adopt accrual accounting. The timeline set in the law was very ambitious, as the reform was to be implemented by end of 2009. However, additional time was necessary to finalise the reform: The first consolidated financial statements for the federal level were indeed published in 2015 only.[4]

Co-ordinating the federal, State, and local levels was one of the main challenges of the preparation phase. Overall, the main challenge faced by the authorities was to find a common ground for federal, State, and local practitioners, which historically followed different accounting laws, principles, and procedures. Therefore, realising the changes to existing entity-specific, State, and local laws, regulations and accounting standards took a long time.

Another challenge consisted in identifying officials for monitoring the reform, and leading changes. The authorities spent significant time bringing together a representative reform monitoring team, and defining its roles and responsibilities. Another difficulty was to identify resources with the relevant knowledge and capacities for developing new accounting manuals and procedures, and delivering training to other officials. Once the reform was rolled-out, another difficulty was to find highly-qualified professionals for preparing the consolidated financial statements.

Last, developing a new IT system took longer than initially expected. Bringing all users together to define the design and functional requirements of the accounting IT system was difficult. During the pre-rollout and roll-out phases, new developments and modifications to the IT system had to be realised, which generated higher costs than expected.

Transparency, accountability, and awareness on the state of public finances are the core benefits from the reform. However, accrual information is not used for annual budgeting and macro fiscal forecasting, and financial analysis of public sector financial accounts is still in infancy. Likewise, assets and liabilities management has not improved so far. The authorities believe that should the IT system deliver reports more tailored to the managers' needs, these benefits could be achieved. Improvements to the IT system are expected, though, one of the main on-going project being to develop automatic reconciliations between data from the budget department, treasury, and banks.

Notes

1. The authorisation to raise revenue is given by the Senate and Parliament, while the authorisation to incur expenses is given by the Parliament only.
2. There are around 100 public enterprises in Mexico, including PEMEX, the national oil company.
3. Monthly financial reports are also prepared, and are published on a quarterly basis
4. There is no plan to establish whole of public sector financial statements - that is to consolidate the federal, regional, and local levels.

Netherlands

Preparation basis and coverage of the budget and financial reports

The government's budget and annual report are established on a cash and multi-year commitments basis. The central government is using a cash and commitments bookkeeping system, with two exceptions: Departmental agencies that use the accrual basis, and expenditures related to "interest payments on central government debt", which is presented on accrual basis. The budget and annual report present the government's current and capital expenditures (i.e., cash payments), revenue (cash receipts, including financing flows), debt, cash balances at bank, guarantees, and multi-year commitments. Expenditures and revenues for each of the line ministries and *High Councils of State* are presented in chapters. The budget and annual report are both presented to the Parliament, and are fully comparable. A supplementary general government balance sheet is disclosed in the annual report of the central government. The balance sheet covers the central government, the social security funds (including health care), the local governments, and the government non-profit institutions. It is prepared by the Statistical Office, based on entities' individual financial reports (including national public agencies, which establish their accounts on an accrual basis). This balance sheet is relatively comprehensive, and assets and liabilities are measured according to the rules and principles applicable for European statistics (for example, market value for assets).

The Legislature authorises the central government expenditures and revenues, multi-year commitments, and debt. Annual appropriation of all central government transactions (e.g. expenditures and tax revenues) is required, including entitlements granted under legislations separate from the budget (for example, entitlements to social security funds (including health care). The legislature authorises also all commitments to be taken on in the budget year, including if the commitments leads to expenditure in a later year. Finally, the legislature also approves the debt refinancing.

The budget and year-end financial report cover the central government. In the Netherlands, the law requires that ministries, national public agencies, and the High Councils of State be covered in the financial reports.

Standard setting and audit arrangements

Accounting standards are set by the Ministry of Finance (MoF). The Government Accounts Act (*Comptabiliteitswet*) sets out broad requirements with regards to central government budgeting and accounting systems. In line with the legal requirements, the MoF sets out detailed rules - tailor made for the government - for recording cash transactions in the bookkeeping system in line ministries (cash-entitlements recording) and departmental agencies (accrual or cash recording).

The annual report is submitted to the Internal Audit Department (IAD) and the SAI for audits. The departmental annual reports are audited by the IAD. Also IT-systems and processes can be audited by the IAD. The SAI reviews the work of the IAD, and reports its findings to the Dutch Parliament.

Status of accruals reform(s)

The adoption of accrual accounting is not considered for the central government. The Dutch central government has weighted the advantages and drawbacks of accrual budgeting and accounting a number of times over the last years. This led to a growing number of public entities (in particular agencies) adopting the accrual basis of accounting. However, as cash-based appropriations are perceived as giving the most relevant information for the budget process and giving the indispensable control on the public finances, the Government decided that the budget and annual report of central government should remain on a cash-basis.

New Zealand

Preparation basis and coverage of the budget and financial reports

The budget and financial statements are prepared on an accrual basis, with supplementary budgetary and management information provided in additional statements:

- All assets and liabilities are recorded in the balance sheet (except for natural resources), revenue and expenditures are recorded on a full accrual basis, including losses arising from revaluation of these assets and liabilities (if any). Assets are measured at market value (tax receivables and lands and non-specialist buildings) or replacement cost (specialist assets, infrastructure, defence and heritage assets). Contingent assets and liabilities are also disclosed in the notes to the financial statements, as well as commitments and specific fiscal risks[1] (the later in the budget only).

- All key statements and disclosures are presented in the budget and *Financial Statements of the Government of New Zealand*. In addition to the budget, the Government establishes a *Statement of specific fiscal risks, contingent liabilities and contingent assets*, and core *Crown expense tables*. The financial statements include a *Statement of Expenses or Capital Expenditure Incurred in Emergencies*, *Statement of Unappropriated Expenditure*, and *Statement of Trust Money*, as well as additional fiscal indicator analysis and information on State-owned enterprises and Crown entities. The Government also prepares a management commentary, and started publishing more recently an *Investment Statement* that measures its performance in managing the Crown's balance sheet.

The legislature authorises current and capital expenditures on an accrual basis. The budget, which defines the government's annual plan for revenues, expenses, assets and liabilities, is accompanied by Estimates of Appropriations. These estimates state the Government objectives and outcomes in relation with the forecasted revenues expenses, and capital acquisitions, and detail by department and agency the appropriations and expected outputs - including output-based appropriations - for approval by the Legislature. Appropriations are granted for current expenses and capital expenditures and expressed on an accrual basis.

The budget and financial statements present a consolidated view of public entities controlled by the central government. The budget and financial statements cover all entities that are considered controlled by the central Government - that is the ministries, departments, offices of Parliament, Crown entities, and State-owned enterprises, and the Central Bank. As charts of accounts and accounting principles have not been harmonised, these entities prepare a reporting package, for budget updates, monthly reporting and at year-end for consolidation purposes. The local governments (Territories), which provide various public services financed by local fees and taxes, are independent from the central government and therefore not consolidated.

Standard setting and audit arrangements

The New Zealand Accounting Standards Board (NZASB), an independent body, sets IPSASs-based national accounting standards for the public sector. For developing the national accounting framework for the public sector, the Government has tasked the NZASB with transposing IPSASs, after considering their relevance in the New Zealand context. Before transposing IPSAS into the national framework, the NZASB can modify the standards to suit the local circumstances. Where IPSASs do not provide any guidance (for example, insurance contracts), the NZASB refers to IFRS. Once a standard is approved by the NZASB, it is deemed a regulation (i.e. regarded as secondary legislation). As the standards are principle based, more detailed guidance is provided in Treasury regulations and circulars.

The government's financial reports are audited by the SAI. The Controller and Auditor-General gives annually an opinion on whether financial statements give a true and fair view of the Government's finances, in compliance with international auditing standards. The opinion on the latest Financial Statements was unqualified.

Status of accruals reform(s)

New Zealand completed its transition to accrual budgeting and accounting in six years, as part of a broader set of reforms. The Public Finance Act of 1989 instituted the move towards a new public sector financial management system and, in particular, a performance based accountability framework. In this context, accrual reporting was seen as a tool for better measuring the financial performance of department and agencies, and it was considered that budgeting should consequently transition to a full accrual basis to provide a direct link between the budget, financial reports, and performance evaluation. The accrual budgeting and accounting reform was monitored by the Treasury, from 1988 to 1994. The six-year transition period is perceived a posteriori as appropriate, as it created both a challenging and manageable timeframe for undertaking all necessary operational tasks.

The reform preparation and implementation did not carry any major challenge, except for assets inventory and valuation. The main preparation challenge was to establish the opening balance sheet, in particular with regards to assets inventory and measurement. The preparers and auditors collaborated for establishing registers, determining the ownership of various assets, and reconciling various ledgers. One important aspect of the successful transition to accrual in New Zealand is the early awareness to the critical role of experienced and qualified staff, and leveraging systems and practices from the private sector. For example, the accounting standards and accompanying manuals were developed with the support of professional accountants, and, with regards to IT systems, the use of corporate systems prove effective. The authorities also consider that the adoption of IPSAS, in more recent years, has simplified further the process of developing guidance and manuals as the IPSASB's Conceptual Framework for General Purpose Financial Reporting by Public-Sector entities is well aligned with the needs of users of the budget documentation and Financial Statements of Government.

The benefits of the reforms are fully achieved. All the expected benefits, in terms of transparency and performance based accountability evaluation have been achieved. One specific aspect of the reform implemented in New Zealand is that fiscal forecasts and targets, annual budgets, financial statements are all prepared on a similar basis - that is on an accrual basis - which has helped achieving the complete shift from cash to accrual in public management. Innovations and improvements continue, with, for example, the publication of the 'actuarially determined future liability for welfare payments', as a basis for determining the impact of social investment initiatives. With regards to performance evaluation, a number of cost measures ratios are benchmarked through the Benchmarking of Administrative and Support Systems process.

Note

1. Specific Fiscal Risks are those government decisions and other circumstances known to the Government at the date of finalisation of the fiscal forecasts that may have a material effect on the fiscal and economic outlook, but are not certain enough in timing or amount to include in the fiscal forecasts

Norway

Preparation basis and coverage of the budget and financial reports

The government's budget and year-end financial report are established on a cash and multi-year commitments basis. The cash basis budget and year-end financial report present the government's current and capital expenditures (i.e., cash payments), cash receipts, and multi-year commitments. In addition, civil service and military pension liabilities and natural resources assets are disclosed in the Budget Bill, and the government's cash balances, financial debt, tax receivables, land and buildings, and guarantees are presented in the year-end financial report.[1] Agencies can prepare on a voluntary basis accrual basis financial statements, which are supplementary information to their mandatory cash basis financial reports.[2] The legislature - the *Storting* - authorises the annual capital and current expenditure, and multi-year commitments. When the Government's policies create multi-year financial obligations for the State, future payments may be appropriated on the year the commitment is made and transferred to a dedicated fund.[3]

The budget and year-end financial report are established at the central government's level. The Government's financial report covers ministries, parliamentary institutions, and the government agencies. The social security fund (*Folketrygden*) is also consolidated in the budget and the financial statement showing the transfers from the fund as expenditures in Government's financial report.

Standard setting and audit arrangements

Cash and accrual accounting standards are set by the MoF. The MoF regulations and circulars establish mandatory budgeting and accounting principles, as well as a chart of accounts, for central government public entities. In addition, the MoF has more recently developed non mandatory accrual basis public sector accounting standards (the SRS). These standards are derived from the national accounting standards for the private sector, which are broadly aligned with IFRS. SRS are to be implemented by those entities that prepare accrual based financial statements on a voluntary basis.

An annual compliance audit is undertaken by the SAI. The SAI performs an annual compliance audit and establishes a report, which is presented to the Parliament. The SAI also realises performance audits in public entities.

Status of accruals reform(s)

Norway is not considering adopting accrual accounting. A government-appointed commission has recommended that accrual accounting be made mandatory for internal reporting purpose, in all central government agencies, as supplementary information to cash reports. If so, in the longer run more accrual information may be disclosed year-end fiscal report, which will however remain on a cash-basis.[4]

Notes

1. The pension liabilities were not disclosed in the 2016 Budget Bill, though, due to measurement issues.
2. As of today, 77 out of 220 ministries and agencies do so.
3. One example is student loans that will be given as grants when the student has passed his/hers exams. Other examples are funds for covering expected losses on given guarantees.
4. The commission's proposals are on a public hearing with deadline 1 March 2016.

Poland

Preparation basis and coverage of the budget and financial reports

The budget and budget execution reports are prepared on cash basis. The Budget Act is composed of a cash basis budget (*Expenditures and Revenues of the State Budget*), which presents the Government's annual payments and receipts and related financing gap, and an appendix (*Justification to the Budget*). The latter includes, among other information on public finances, some accrual elements, such as the stock of public debt and Treasury receivables. On that basis, the Legislature authorises the State current and capital expenses. Budget execution reports produced in year and at year end are prepared on a similar basis than the budget.

Year-end financial statements are prepared on accrual basis. The financial statements include all key statements and disclosures - except for the Cash Flow Statement. All assets, liabilities, expenses, revenues, and contingent liabilities are reported or reported in the financial statements, except for natural resources. Assets are measured at historical cost.

The budget and year-end financial report cover the budgetary central government. The State budget covers all expenditures of all entities acting at the country level: ministries, agencies, institutes, courts, special purpose funds, state donations for education, health, culture and local entities etc. Local entities (municipalities) are independent and they have their own budgets. Individual financial statements are established by each public sector entity both at local and central level and those statements are not consolidated.

Standard setting and audit arrangements

Accounting standards are enacted in laws and regulations. The Accounting Act sets out the general principles and rules on accounting for all entities (both in public and private sector). The MoF also issues a regulation for the core public sector entities (those without legal personality who incur liabilities on behalf of the state treasury or local budget). The regulation sets up specific public sector accounting rules (e.g. registration of the budgetary flows), standardised chart of accounts, standardised forms of financial statements (balance, P&L, changes in funds/equity and notes) as well as some simplifications (for example on provisions for employee benefits).

The Supreme Audit Institution audits annually the budget execution. The Polish Constitution requires the *Najwyższa Izba Kontroli* (NIK) to carry out annual audits on budget execution in central government public entities. The findings of these audits are presented in a report that is sent to the audited executive level and the lower chamber of Parliament (*Seym*). Budgets of other public entities are audited by local audit institutions. This is a control on law compliance and economic efficiency.

Status of accruals reform(s)

The transition to accrual accounting is completed. The public accounting reform took place in the 1990s: Changes in the political and economic systems in Poland drove evolutions in public sector management. In the accounting area, a new accrual basis framework was adopted for both the private and public sectors. The implementation of the new accounting system was monitored by the MoF. The main challenges consisted in adapting the existing regulations; setting a reform team; realising the inventories of assets and liabilities; and managing the transition period. Currently Poland is analysing the differences between the national accrual system and IPSAS. Some adjustments may be considered if the cost-benefit ratio is positive.

Despite accrual accounting dating back to the 1990s, expected benefits have not been achieved yet. Benefits with regards to accountability, transparency, and public management efficiency are partially achieved. The co-existence of two accounting systems may explain the lack of interest for the year-end financial statements on accrual basis, and predominance, in the budget process, of the cash-basis reports.

Portugal

Preparation basis and coverage of the budget and financial reports

The year-end financial report is prepared on both cash and cash transitioning to accruals bases. The *General State Accounts* are established annually by the MoF. They include a commentary of year-end fiscal figures, a cash basis outturn, and partial consolidated financial statements for the Social Security Sector. With regards to the central government, assets and liabilities are not reported exhaustively yet. In particular, tax receivables, PPPs related assets and liabilities, financial instruments (including derivatives), civil service pensions. In the individual financial statements of central government entities, fixed assets and social benefits are reported, with fixed assets valued at historical cost.

The budget and year-end financial report cover the central government, including social security funds. As required by the Budget Framework Law, the budget and General State Accounts include all of the Integrated Services (SIs), the Autonomous Funds and Agencies (SFAs), and the Social Security. The consolidation of the General State Accounts is realized semi-manually by the MoF, based on available information. The General State Accounts also includes aggregated figures for regional and local government entities. The Social Security establishes individual consolidated financial statements.

Standard setting and audit arrangements

Accounting standards are enacted in laws and regulations. The law and the Decree law of budget execution set out, for general government public entities, the reporting obligations towards the MoF and define the applicable accounting framework. The MoF is responsible for the technical preparation of laws concerning the budget and accounting, and also for enacting circulars that define precisely the accounting requirements for the public sector. The national standards are in a transition phase to IPSASs, which will be adopted by 2017 (see below).

The Supreme Audit Institution audits annually the budget execution. Following a compliance audit, the Court of Auditors (CoA) issues annually an Opinion on the General State Accounts. This report is issued in accordance with the *Court of Accounts Organization and Procedure Act*. The report includes findings on the legality of the central government's budgetary execution, and also aims to contribute to the improvement of the reliability and accuracy of the General State Account. The CoA also issues an opinion on whether the Social Security consolidated financial statements present a true and fair view of its economic and financial situation. The financial statements of local governments are audited by professional audit firms.

Status of accruals reform(s)

Following the revision of the Budget Framework Law and Accounting Law, Portugal is starting its accrual accounting reform. A new Budget Framework Law has been adopted in September 2015, which launches a number of reforms in the budgeting and accounting areas. It includes an integrated system of budgeting with a new budget cycle, budget programmes, a medium-term perspective, and a gradual move to accrual accounting. The law requires also that the Government starts establishing a balance sheet presenting all assets and liabilities and prepares consolidated financial statements (prospective and at year-end), on which the Court of Auditors will give an opinion in accordance with international standards on auditing. In addition, all public entities should use IPSASs for establishing their financial statements starting from 2017. The implementation of the reform will be monitored by the MoF and audit entities.

Preparations for the reform have just started, and the main challenge, so far, has been to design the new functional requirements of the IT system. In addition to the planned reforms, Portugal has recently started publishing a "Citizen Budget" and "Citizen Accounts", with the objective of better communicating with the public at large about public policies and resources allocation, results achieved, and the state of public finances.

Slovak Republic

Preparation basis and coverage of the budget and financial reports

The State budget is prepared on a cash basis. The budget bill presents the federal government's current and capital expenditures (i.e., cash payments), cash receipts, and cash balances at bank. In addition, since 2013, contingent liabilities, guarantees, and pension liabilities are disclosed in the budget documentation. The legislature authorises the capital and current expenditures.

The year-end financial statements are prepared on an accrual basis. The financial statements are composed of a balance sheet, income statement, and notes. The comparison of budget and actuals, and table on changes in net assets are disclosed in the notes to the financial statements, but the financial statements do not include a cash flow statement. Fixed assets are reported and valued at historical cost. Tax receivables are measured at nominal value. Natural resources and heritage assets are not recorded, though, as their value cannot be measured reliably. The accounting treatment for pensions and social benefits and PPP liabilities is not aligned with international standards: With regards to pensions and social benefits, only yearly payments are reported in the operating statement and budget execution reports, and PPP liabilities are recorded for the amount that is due and payable to the private operator for the construction of the asset and services.

The State budget and year-end financial statements do not have the same coverage. The State budget presents the State revenues, expenditures of 'budgetary organisations' that are financed exclusively by State revenues (such as ministries), and transfers to other public entities at the central or local levels. The financial statements cover the whole of the public sector entities - that is budgetary organisations, contributory organisations that receive transfers or another public funding (such as social funds), municipalities and higher territorial units, and the state owned corporations (SOEs). It is to be noted that the authorities consolidate the whole of the public sector despite local government not being controlled by the central government.

There are three levels of consolidated financial statements, from budgetary central government to public sector:

- Ministries, higher territorial unit, and municipalities prepare financial statements consolidating all the public entities they control (budgetary organisations, contributory organisations, or public sector enterprises) - this is the first level of consolidation;
- The National Reporting Section of MoF prepares consolidated financial statements for the central government - this is the second level of consolidation;
- The National Reporting Section of MoF also prepares the financial statements for the whole of the public sector - this is the final level of consolidation.

Accounting practices have been harmonised to allow for the consolidation of the public sector. Since 2008, most central government entities use the same chart of accounts and accounting standards; however, as accounting practices have not been harmonised for the whole public sector, reporting packages are prepared at year-end and consolidated under a dedicated IT system.

Standard setting and audit arrangements

Accounting standards are set by the MoF. The broad principles for budgeting and accounting are set in the law (for example, in the Act n°431/2002 on Accounting), and the MoF is tasked with preparing regulations with more detailed guidance consistent with the legal requirements. The regulations are specific to each category of public entities. Since 2008, the national accounting standards for the public sector are based on IPSAS, with some divergences (for example, the Slovak public sector accounting standards do not contain rules for discounting long term provisions).

The central government's financial statements are audited by the SAI. The Supreme Audit Office of the Republic of Slovakia performs an annual financial audit of the consolidated financial statements for the central government (second level of consolidation) despite not auditing the individual financial statements on the consolidated entities. Its latest report included observations on the weaknesses of internal control, the reliability of the inventory and measurement of fixed assets and the general quality of the accounting data. In addition, some compliance audits are regularly performed on public entities.

Status of accruals reform(s)

The Slovak republic completed its accrual accounting reform about eight years. The accounting reform was part of a wider "Public Financial Management" reform that started in 1998 and was aimed at strengthening institutions with regards to budgeting, expenditure management, and financial reporting. The public sector accounting reform was specifically aimed at *i)* improving the accounting system as a whole (processes, financial controls, etc.), *ii)* providing better and more regular information to senior officials; and *iii)* preparing financial statements and other fiscal reports according to international standards in order to meet the needs of all external stakeholders (Parliament, foreign investors, EUROSTAT, International Monetary Fund, etc.).

The reform preparation was organised around three components[1]:

- First, organisation of the project and the modernisation of the accounting system, including the roll-out of a new State Treasury IT system for processing payments (improvements to the IT systems are on-going, and the authorities aim at rolling out a single accounting system for the central government) ;
- Second, the setting of new accounting standards based on IPSAS;
- Third, the delivery of trainings in four key areas: *i)* basics of accrual accounting, *ii)* national accounting standards based on IPSAS, *iii)* consolidation and reporting techniques and (iv) IPSASs - for a selected group of specialists.

The main challenges were met at the preparation phase for adapting existing laws and regulations, and delivering the training to around 6 500 accountants.

Note

1. This was implemented with technical assistance from the World Bank.

Slovenia

Preparation basis and coverage of the budget and financial reports

The State budget is prepared on a cash basis. The budget bill comprises a statement that presents the current and capital expenditures (i.e., cash payments), cash receipts, and a financing statement, which presents the borrowing needs and repayments of debt. The legislature authorises the capital and current expenditures.

The year-end financial report is prepared on a cash basis, with accrual elements. The financial report is composed of a balance sheet, cash-flow statement, and notes. Comments on the financial situation are also provided. The balance sheet is relatively comprehensive: For example, tax receivables, fixed assets, and derivatives are reported. Fixed assets are measured at historical cost, and are therefore reported only when documentation is available to estimate that cost.

The coverage of the year-end financial report is wider than the coverage of the State budget. In compliance with legal requirements, the State budget covers the ministries and other government bodies; social security funds; and local and regional governments. In addition to the above, the year-end financial report covers a number of public entities, such as schools, hospitals, universities. These entities use similar charts of accounts and accounting principles. Their accounts are maintained and consolidated under a shared IT system (except for some municipalities and the social security funds).

Standard setting and audit arrangements

The requirements applying to the budget and financial report's preparation are set in the legal framework. The Slovene Law on Accounting was revised back in1999. The law requires entities within the State budget to maintain their accounts on a cash basis, and mentions the international statistics manual (GFSM) as a reference. The assets and liabilities reported in the balance sheet are reported and measured in compliance with IFRS. Detailed guidance on budgeting and accounting principles is provided in MoF regulations and circulars.

The year-end financial report is audited by the Supreme Audit Institution (SAI). The Court of Auditors performs compliance, financial, performance, and IT audits. The frequency of these audits differs for each category of public entities. The Government year-end financial report is audited annually, in compliance with international audit standards. The last audit resulted in a qualified opinion, due to issues with intra-group reconciliations, and the boundaries of the financial report.

Status of accruals reform(s)

Slovenia plans to adopt accrual accounting by 2022. The MoF prepares a revision to the Slovene Law on Accounting. The revised law would require all entities within the State budget to maintain their accounts both on a cash basis (for establishing budget execution reports) and on an accrual basis (for establishing financial accounts) by 2022.

The authorities do not anticipate major challenges. The Public Accounting Directorate would be responsible for the reform implementation. With regards to IT, entities are already using a shared system, and practices are relatively harmonised. The MoF is however aware that performing inventories and delivering training will be time consuming.

Spain

Preparation basis and coverage of the budget and financial reports

The budget is prepared on cash basis. The budget presents expenditures and revenues on cash basis, the corresponding financing gap, and the cash balances at bank. The budget is structured as follows: Economic classification and organisational allocations of revenues and expenditures, and expenditure 'areas', 'policies', and 'programmes'. The in-year and year-end budget execution reports are prepared on a similar basis. The legislature authorises the current and capital expenses, and establishes limits for the amounts that the government is authorised to borrow during the year.

The year-end financial statements are prepared on accrual basis. The financial statements are composed of a full suite of statements. Assets and liabilities are recorded in the balance sheet, except for natural resources, social benefits, civil service and military pensions, and PPP assets and liabilities, which are presented in a disclosure.[1] Assets are measured at historical cost.

The budget and year-end financial report cover the central government, including social security funds. The budget and consolidated year-end financial statements cover all ministries, autonomous bodies and agencies and the Social Security Funds, which are all controlled by the State:

- In addition to central government entities and social security funds, the budget includes aggregated figures for independent regional and local governments, and the general government as a whole.[2] In addition, spending ministries are required to produce budgetary documentation that group the programs delivered by their operational divisions, including those performed by agencies, corporations or public enterprises with a functional dependency on the ministry;

- The consolidated financial statements are established based on reporting packages prepared annually by central government entities and social security funds, as their individual financial statements are not established under similar principles and charts of accounts. The consolidation is undertaken by the MoF, under an IT system developed in-house.

Standard setting and audit arrangements

Accounting standards are set out by the MoF and are based on IPSASs. Requirements regarding applying to budget and financial reports preparation are set out in laws (General Budgetary Law) and regulations issued by the MoF (2010 General Government Accounting Plan - GGCA). In particular, the GGCA includes a conceptual framework, accounting standards, layouts for annual accounts, charts of accounts and definitions. The accounting principles set out in the GGCA are based on IPSAS, with some deviations.

The SAI audits annually the budget execution. For the central government, the functions of auditing are vested in two institutions: the General Audit Office (*Intervención General de la Administración del Estado* - IGAE) and the Court of Auditors (*Tribunal de Cuentas*). Audits are focused on controlling the compliance and legally of financial transactions. The individual financial statements of public entities other than the ministries are submitted to a financial audit performed by the Court of Auditors, accounting firms, or regional Court of Audits.

Status of accruals reform(s)

Spain completed its accrual accounting reform progressively, in about 25 years. The accrual accounting reform for the public sector started in the 1980s, and followed a gradual path: In 1986, the GGCA required that public entities maintain double entry book-keeping; in 1990, accrual accounting principles were introduced in the public accounting framework; and in 2007 and 2010, the GGCA was revised to adopt full accrual accounting principles in the public sector. The reform was sponsored by the MoF, and monitored by the General Audit Office (*Intervención General de la Administración* del Estado – IGAE).

The authorities consider that all tasks at the preparation and implementation stages were highly challenging, in the context of limited resources:

- Adapting the legal framework, developing accounting standards, and developing manuals and guidance: The IGAE relied on working groups to undertake these tasks;
- Finding competencies and building knowledge: The IGAE developed and delivered internal training programmes;
- Performing inventories and valuations: This has been achieved progressively, with pilots and tests;
- Delivering high quality accounting data: An IT system was developed internally and the internal control environment strengthened;
- Consolidating the financial statements: The number of intra-group eliminations was increased over time.

Benefits have been fully achieved. Better financial information and standardisation of business processes have been achieved, due mainly to the roll-out of a new IT system, which can produce real-time accounting data. Accountability and transparency have been strengthened (the financial statements are published on the MoF's website). The analysis on the state of public finances has been reinforced too, and a number of financial, budgetary, and management ratios are now discussed in the notes to the financial statements.[3]

Notes

1. Accounting standards on social benefits and pensions should be enacted soon, and information on PPPs includes objective and duration of the contract, transfers and grants commitments, and costs.
2. Each local and regional government also prepares an individual budget.
3. The management ratios include liquidity ratios, debt ratios, revenues and expenses structure ratios.

Sweden

Preparation basis and coverage of the budget and financial reports

Budget and budget execution report mix elements reported on cash and accrual bases. Expenditures and revenues are presented differently depending on their nature:

- Transfers and grants and revenue from EU funds are presented on a cash basis;
- Infrastructure assets are presented on a cost basis (acquisition cost);
- Taxes, fees, other income, and administrative expenditure are presented on an accrual basis - that is the year which the revenue or expense belongs to (independently from the payment).

Despite some elements of the budget being recorded on accrual basis, the budget balance is presented on a full cash basis.[1] The budget is composed of 27 expenditure areas, nine income headings, and shows the change in net loans and credits, and the legislature authorises the current and capital expenses for each expenditure area. Budget execution reports are presented on a similar basis than the budget and published monthly.

The year-end financial statements are prepared on accrual basis. The Annual Report, established at year-end by the Swedish National Financial Management Agency (*Ekonomistyrningverket-* ESV), includes all key statements and disclosures. It also includes a bridge table between the statement of financial performance and annual budget execution report and detailed information on the national debt and Government's guarantees, as well a Government comment. In principle all assets and liabilities are recorded in the balance sheet, except for future payments attributable to social benefits.[2] Revenue and expenditures are recorded on a full accrual basis, including losses arising from revaluation of these assets and liabilities (if any). Assets are measured at historical cost. Taxes are accrued using macro-economic models. Financial assets and liabilities are measured at amortised cost. Financial Instruments that held for generating yield or increases in value are measured at fair value.

The budget and year-end financial statements cover the central government, as legally required:

- The Budget Bill covers the Parliament, ministries, and some 250 government agencies. The pension system is not included in the budget, with the exception of the old-age pensions paid out by the Swedish Social Insurance Agencies. Local government and SOEs are not covered in the budget, but the grants they receive are individually disclosed;
- The Annual Report has a similar coverage than the budget. In addition, in the financial statements, the SOEs equity value is reported in the balance sheet, with a note detailing the value of each corporation. With regards to the consolidation, financial reporting requirements for agencies are issued by the ESV (they include, for example, guidance for reconciling intra-governmental transactions). As the

agencies' charts of accounts are not harmonised, their accounts must be converted to a mandatory set of reporting codes before being consolidated by the ESV under a dedicated IT system.

Standard setting and audit arrangements

Accounting standards are set by the Government. Broad accounting principles are set out in the law, and more detailed principles are enacted by the Government in regulations. The budget law states the fundamental accounting principles and which financial statements and other descriptive parts should be included in the CG annual report for the consolidated level. The government ordinances regulate the content of the agencies' annual reports and go further into how different items in the financial statements should be classified and measured by the agencies. ESV submits proposals for changes in the government ordinances and issue recommendations how the regulations should be interpreted. The third level is the ESV regulations where ESV regulates the form for financial statements for the agencies, and many detailed rules about which information should be included in notes and disclosures.

The Supreme Audit Institution audits annually both the Central government Annual Report and the agencies' individual annual reports including financial statements. The Swedish National Audit Office (SNAO) gives an opinion on whether the accounts are true and fair (financial audit) and the financial law, ordinance and regulations have been respected (compliance audit).[3] The SNAO's opinion on the consolidated financial statements for the central government is unqualified.

Status of accruals reform(s)

Sweden completed its transition to accrual accounting in about 15 years. The accrual accounting reform was initiated in 1990s, when the move to results-based management for agencies created the need for a better measurement of their costs. Another motivation was to be able to recruit professional accountants. The scope and extent of the "accrual accounting reform" has been extended over time (in particular, accrual accounting was adopted at the ministries' level after it was implemented in agencies), and the transition to accrual accounting in the public sector was therefore implemented in successive steps. This very long timeframe makes it difficult to identify specific challenges with regards to the preparation and implementation of the reform. The Government and ESV actually consider that improvements to the consolidated and individual financial statements are still possible, and the reform effort is therefore constant.

The expected benefits have been achieved partially. Questions remain about the usefulness of the accrual based financial statements for macro-fiscal forecasting, and in the political debate. The budget balance and net lending, measured according to statistical standards, remain indeed the key fiscal figures in Sweden, and focus most of the political and public attention. In addition, to date, accrual accounting and consolidated financial statements are little used for managerial planning, budgetary decision making, or even control purpose at the State level.

Notes

1. The restatement of the balance is done using cash correction items.
2. Social benefits are recorded on a cash basis and only the annual cash outflows appear in the operating statement, cash flows statement, and budget outturn. Natural resources and heritage assets are only partly reported in the balance sheet. There are also some exceptions for heritage assets and land acquired before 2000.
3. However some of the information provided of the Annual Report (such as the performance information) cannot be audited according international audit standards. For this reason the SNAO's opinion on the Annual Report has a limited scope.

Switzerland

Preparation basis and coverage of the budget and financial reports

The federal government (the Confederation) prepares its budget and year-end financial report on an accrual basis:

- The financial reports are composed of a full set of statements and notes, as required by international standards. All statements are presented in accordance with the requirements of IPSAS, and the budget statement is presented on the basis of the COFOG (Classification of Functions of Government);

- Assets and liabilities are reported in accordance with the requirements of IPSASs, with limited deviations. For example, fixed assets are valued at cost, and tax receivables are measured at market value. Assets and liabilities may however not be reported where no accounting treatment has been defined yet: This is the case for natural resources, heritage assets, and social benefits liabilities.[1] Civil and military service pensions are treated as contingent liabilities: They are measured annually (according to the methods prescribed in IPSAS 25 Employee benefits) and disclosed in the notes to the financial statements. Defence assets and inventories are not reported, to avoid discrepancies between the financial statements and statistics.[2]

Appropriations are voted on current and capital expenditures, and commitments. Balance sheet items, such as fixed assets, are not subject to budgeting. With regards to expenditure, the Parliament votes two types of credits: the cash items (e.g. salaries, operating and capital expenditure), and non-cash items, which represent book entries only with no flow of money (e.g. depreciation or provisions).[3]

The Confederation financial reports cover all federal entities, which are listed in the law. These include the Confederation's departments, agencies, and authorities. These entities use a harmonised chart of accounts and overarching accounting principles based on IPSAS for establishing their individual financial statements. The system automatically consolidates these individual financial statements into the Confederation financial report.

Standard Setting and Audit Arrangements

The requirements applying to the budget and financial reports' preparation are set out in laws and regulations. In particular, the law requires the Confederation to prepare its budget and financial reports in accordance with IPSASs, and only the Federal Council (i.e., the federal government) can authorise deviations.

The year-end financial reported is submitted to an audit by the Swiss Federal Audit Office (SFAO). The audit performed does follow Swiss Audit Standards, an equivalent to the International Audit Standards (ISA). The SFAO delivered an unqualified audit opinion on the latest year-end financial statements. It highlighted several key audit matters, for example the valuation of the loan granted to the unemployment insurance and the FinPT fund, and the audit arrangement for the direct federal tax.

Status of Accruals Reform(s)

The Confederation has completed its transition to accrual budgeting and accounting. The reform was initiated in the 2000s, by the Director General of the Swiss Federal Finance Administration with the support of the Minister of Finance, Government, and Parliament. Its objective was to 'close the gap' between the Federation and cantons in terms of financial transparency. The Federal Budget Act was revised after several consultations between the administration and politicians.

Challenges were focused in three main areas during the preparation and implementation phases:

- Development of the IT system: Developing the IT system required a strong project organisation, with cost control as one of the main area of attention. Another challenge was find staff with the required technical competences, and to bring all stakeholders on board;

- Human resources management: Authorities had to develop the knowledge and competencies of officials with regards to accrual budgeting and accounting, which required creating high level educational material;

- Operational organisation: This included defining realistic goals in terms of timeframe for the reform, monitoring and assisting the agencies during the inventory of assets, and co-operating with the Comptroller's office.

Expected benefits were almost fully achieved, but interest in the accrual financial information remains limited. Transparency and accountability have been strengthened as expected. However, questions remain on the usefulness of accrual data remains, in particular with regards to fiscal decision making and forecasting. In addition, the public awareness to public finances issues remains limited. To address this, the government made the financial statements more easily available to the public using the new information technologies.

Notes

1. There are no PPP arrangements at the Confederation level.
2. At the time of the introduction of IPSAS in 2007, statistics didn't require the recognition of defence assets. From 2017 the Swiss Confederation is planning to recognise them as the statistical requirements have changed since then.
3. Some of these non-cash items may result in internal service charges, with an effect on credits in a given department or unit's budget.

Turkey

Preparation basis and coverage of the budget and financial reports

The budget is prepared on cash basis. The budget presents all expenditures (current and capital) and revenues on cash basis, which are authorised by the legislature annually. The budget comprises the current and capital transfers to social security institutions and local government (including tax shares), which are subject to authorisation in the central government budget process. The budget is presented using four classifications: Institutional, functional, financing, and economical.

The year-end financial report is prepared on an accrual basis. The financial report comprises a balance sheet, operating statement, statement of cash flow, and disclosures. Assets and liabilities are reported, with an exception of civil and military service pensions and social benefits, natural resources and heritage assets.

The budget covers the central government, while the financial statements cover the general government:

- The central government budget consists of three parts: *i)* the general budget agencies: Ministries and agencies directly affiliated to ministries; *ii)* special budget agencies: Agencies belonging to the central government but with some degree of autonomy; and *iii)* regulatory and supervisory agencies: Agencies belonging to the central government but with a larger degree of autonomy. Supplementary information on expenditures, revenues and balance of social security institutions and local governments is comprised in the budget documentation of the central government and submitted to parliament, but not for the purpose of authorisation;

- The year-end financial report covers the entities mentioned above, as well as the social security institutions and local governments. The consolidation scope is determined based on the control approach, as set out in international statistical frameworks.[1] The Ministry of Finance's General Directorate of Public Accounts has established a uniform accounting system for the general government. It is also responsible for compiling, consolidating and disseminating accounting data and financial statements for the central government on a monthly basis, and general government on a yearly and quarterly basis.[2] For other entities (special budget agencies, regulatory and supervisory agencies, social security institutions and local governments), accounting services are provided by their own accounting units, but they report to the Ministry of Finance. The consolidation is realised using a dedicated IT system.

Standard setting and audit arrangements

Accounting standards are enacted by an independent standard setter. The *Public Financial Management and Control Law* (PFMC), adopted by the Turkish parliament in December 2003 (Law No. 5018, amended in 2005, Law No. 5436), is setting out the overall principles with regards to the budget and accounts preparation. The accounting and reporting standards for general government are set by the *State Accounting Standards Board*, which is established within the Ministry of Finance, as required by Article 49 of the PFMC law. The board consists of representatives from the Turkish Court of Accounts, the Ministry of Finance, the State Planning Organisation, the Treasury, the Higher Education Council, the Ministry of the Interior, and the social security institutions. The standards are aligned, to the extent possible, with IPSAS.

The Supreme Audit Institution audits annually the financial report. External audit is regulated by the law on the Turkish Court of Accounts (TCA). Article 68 of the PFMC Law specifies that the TCA may audit all general government organisations (central government agencies, local governments and social security institutions). The Turkish Constitution mandates that the final accounts law should be submitted to parliament within six months of the end of the fiscal year and that the Court of Accounts shall submit its certification no later than 75 days thereafter. The latest opinion has been qualified, due to issues with intra-group eliminations.

Status of accruals reform(s)

The authorities consider that their transition to accrual accounting is on-going. In 2005, the PMFC Law replaced the outdated 1927 Law on Public Accounting. The Government and Ministry of Finance were the main sponsors of the new law, which introduced accrual accounting, and a provision on general government consolidation. Since the adoption of the law, several steps have been taken towards its full implementation, including the adoption a harmonised chart of accounts and internal control processes for all public entities, and development of a new IT system for financial operations.[3] The reform are almost achieved, despite a number of outstanding issues, in particular, a number of challenges with regards to social security institutions' reporting, and audit qualifications to be addressed. The authorities consider that the Government's transparency and accountability have been increased thanks to the reforms. Other benefits remain however to be achieved, and may be met when all aspects of the accounting reform will be implemented.

Notes

1. European System of Accounts 2010, Government Finance Statistics 2014, and System of National Accounts 2008.
2. Other functions of the General Directorate of Public Accounts include the training and certification of accounting officers.
3. Using a commercial database, the Ministry of Finance developed in-house an automated online accounting system, Say2000i, which has been rolled out in 2002. This online accounting system can produce periodic financial statements without the typical delays of decentralised accounting systems.

United Kingdom

Preparation basis and coverage of the budget and financial reports

The budget and year-end financial statements are prepared on an accruals basis. Central government departments and the majority of individual public sector entities prepare financial statements on an accruals basis, as per International Financial Reporting Standards (IFRS) as adapted for the public sector. Budgets are set on a similar basis. A consolidated set of all public sector entities is produced, known as the *Whole of Government Accounts* (WGA), which are composed of a full suite of accruals based financial statements as per IFRS. There is considerable alignment between departmental accounts, budgets and the WGA. All are prepared on an accruals basis but small differences remain. All assets and liabilities are recorded on balance sheets, except for natural resources and social benefits. Revenue and expenditure are recorded on a full accruals basis. Current value in existing use is the preferred measurement basis for fixed assets.1. In addition to this, at year-end, the Government prepares a Consolidated Statement of Changes in Taxpayers' equity and a management commentary for the WGA.[2]

The legislature authorises current and capital expenses on accrual basis, as well as cash allocations for departments. Each year Parliament gives statutory authority for the consumption of resources, capital spending, and for cash to be drawn from the Consolidated Fund (the government's general bank account at the Bank of England) by Acts of Parliament known as *Supply and Appropriation Acts*. The Estimates should be consistent with UK's fiscal rules[3], which are measured at the level of the public sector. Departments and other public entities' expenditures are controlled against this authority. Estimates and government measures of total public expenditure are on an accruals basis consistent with National Accounts statistical definitions.

The budget and year-end financial statements cover the public sector (so called Whole of Government Accounts). The WGA consolidates the accounts of approximately 5 500 organisations across the public sector that are considered to be controlled by the central government as per the National Accounts - that is the ministries, departments, offices of Parliament, local government entities, and State-owned enterprises (SOEs). As charts of accounts have not been fully harmonised, these entities prepare a reporting package and at year-end for consolidation purposes.

Standard setting and audit arrangements

Accounting standards are set by HMT, advised by an independent advisory board (Financial Reporting Advisory Board - FRAB), and based on IFRS. The accounting framework for central government entities is set out by Her Majesty's Treasury (HMT). The accounts of central government departments and agencies are prepared in accordance with the Government Resources and Accounts Act 2000 (GRAA) and the Government Financial Reporting Manual (FReM) which applies International Financial Reporting Standards (IFRS) as adapted or interpreted for the public sector, and sets out the framework by which departments should prepare their resource accounts.

Local government and NHS accounting standards are set by separate authorities, although there is close working with the Treasury and devolved authorities to ensure that standards are consistent and enable efficient production of WGA.

An independent institution audits annually the Annual Report and Accounts (ARAs) and individual financial statements. The National Audit Office (NAO), led by the Comptroller and Auditor General, gives annually an opinion on whether the WGA, as well as individual accounts of all government departments and many other public sector bodies, give a true and fair view of the government's finances, in compliance with international auditing standards. The opinion on the WGA was qualified since their first publication, due to issues with the consolidation (intra-group eliminations, boundaries of the WGA, qualifications on individual financial statements of consolidated entities) and the quality of the accounting data (including assets inventory and valuation).

Status of accruals reform(s)

The UK completed its transition to resource based budgeting and accrual accounting in about ten years. The adoption of accruals based budgeting and accounting across the whole public sector derived from the motivation across Parliament and government to modernise, enhance accountability and improve decision making. The transition process, and the accompanying accruals based budgeting and accounting arrangements, was led by HMT. It started in 1993 and was concluded in 2002. HMT undertook formal monitoring and assessment of departments' progress through a series of "trigger points" against which progress could be monitored and assessed, and which would allow sufficient time to resolve any problems which emerged. The timescale for implementation was also set to accommodate the scale of systems changes in departments as part of the normal replacement cycle. HMT also used pilots and dry runs to mitigate the risks involved by the reforms (in particular, a dry run public spending review was carried out with departments in 1999, and in-year control arrangements were tested during from 1999 to 2001).

Developing and rolling-out new IT systems were the major challenges of the accruals reform. Before the transition to accruals based accounting, senior departmental management was unaware of the extent of issues with financial information systems - a position exacerbated by a cash system which demanded and offered very little to those not directly involved in its operation. Identifying and evaluating assets and liabilities as part of the opening balance sheet was also a significant challenge, which was factored into timescales. With regards to capacity building, departments were encouraged to spread financial expertise widely among non-professionals. A training network was set up by HMT to disseminate best practice and this turned into a formal committee as implementation came closer. With regards to accounting standard setting, the FRAB was established in 1996 to offer an independent oversight of the Treasury's Resource Accounting Manual, and provided an important focal point for resolving the many difficult accounting issues faced. HMT maintained a high level of stakeholder commitment and buy-in throughout the project. This was achieved through a collaborative approach with major stakeholders, in particular Parliament and the NAO.

The expected benefits have been achieved partially. While there is a wide acknowledgement that additional financial information is now available to the public, and that close alignment of presentation and treatment of financial transactions between Estimates, budgets and accounts has been achieved, the accrual-based information could be developed further. Therefore, a 'Streamlining and Simplifying' project is being implemented in 2015-16 with the aim of making further improvements in reporting financial and nonfinancial information in ARAs, so as to better meet the needs of the users.

Notes

1. Fixed assets are measured at current value in existing use and defence inventories are valued at the lower of cost and net realisable value. However, heritage assets are disclosed when their value cannot be measured reliably; natural resources are not disclosed in the balance sheet, but performance measures are reported against sustainability targets (greenhouse gas emissions, waste minimisation, and use of finite resources).

2. The Statement of Changes in Taxpayers Equity shows the increase or decrease in a department's net assets between the start and end of the financial year. Details of the total parliamentary funding received by departments are shown in this statement. (Source: National Audit Office website).

3. The fiscal rules are the Cyclically-adjusted Current Balance, which measures total public sector expenditure (minus spending on net investment) less public sector current receipts, after adjusting for any spare capacity in the economy, and the Public Sector Net Debt (PSND), which is a measure of the stock of debt that includes the government's financial liabilities (such as government bonds and National Savings and pensions liabilities) less liquid assets. (Source: HMT website).

United States of America

Preparation basis and coverage of the budget and financial reports

The year-end financial statements are prepared on accrual basis. The Department of the Treasury (Treasury), in coordination with the Office of Management and Budget, annually prepares the Financial Report of the United States Government (also called Consolidated Financial report - CFR):

- Most assets and liabilities are recorded in the balance sheet, except for: 1) natural resources (i.e., federal oil and gas resources), which are included in Required Supplementary Information, 2) heritage assets, for which nonfinancial information is disclosed in the notes to the financial statements and 3) social benefits beyond "due and payable" amounts, which are reported in a separate "Statement of Social Insurance" and "Statement of Changes in Social Insurance". Expenses are recorded on a full accrual basis, but revenue is recorded on a modified cash basis. The preferred evaluation method for assets is the historical cost.

- A full suite of accrual basis statements is presented in the CFR. A Statement of Reconciliation of Net Operating Cost to Budget Deficit is prepared in lieu of the statement of comparison of budget and actual amounts is not prepared. In addition to this, a Statement of Long-Term Fiscal Projections (for the federal government as a whole), a Statement of Social Insurance, and a Statement of Changes in Social Insurance (for Social Insurance programmes e.g., Social Security and Medicare) are presented as audited basic financial statements.[1] A management's discussion and analysis is also included in the CFR.

Revenue and expenditures are generally presented on an accrual basis. Expenses are generally recognised when incurred. Non-exchange revenues, including taxes, duties, fines, and penalties, are recognised when collected and adjusted for the change in net measurable and legally collectible amounts receivable. Related refunds and other offsets, including those that are measurable and legally payable, are netted against non-exchange revenue. Exchange (earned) revenue is recognised when the government provides goods and services to the public for a price. Exchange revenue includes user charges such as admission to federal parks and premiums for certain federal insurance. Subsidy expense for direct or guaranteed loans disbursed during a fiscal year is the present value of estimated net cash flows for those loans or guarantees. A subsidy expense also is recognized for modifications made during the year to loans and guarantees outstanding made as of the end of the fiscal year to the subsidy allowances or loan guarantee liability and guarantees outstanding.

Financial statements are established for both for individual federal entities and for the federal government as a whole. The CFR includes the financial status and activities of the executive branch, the legislative branch, and the judicial branch of the government. Entities are consolidated when they meet the criteria set in the Statement of Federal Financial Accounting Concept (SFFAC) No. 2, Entity and Display, which will be superseded by Statement of Federal Financial Accounting Standard (SFFAS) 47, Reporting Entity. SFFAS 47 becomes effective for periods beginning after 30 September 2017 (Fiscal Year 2018 reporting).

Standard setting and audit arrangements

Accounting standards are set by an independent advisory board. The Federal Accounting Standards Advisory Board - (FASAB) promulgates accounting standards for the federal government. These national standards differ from IPSAS on a number of issues. The Office of Management and Budget (Executive Office of the President) and the U.S. Department of the Treasury issue regulations and guidance on budget and financial reports preparation in line with and in support of the FASAB standards.

An independent institution audits annually the government wide consolidated financial report and individual agency financial statements. The Government Accountability Office (GAO) audits annually the CFR, in compliance with generally accepted government auditing standards. Several long-standing material weaknesses and other scope limitations have prevented GAO from being able to express any opinion on the federal government's consolidated financial statements. Issues identified by the GAO include: 1) Certain material weaknesses in internal control and financial reporting at three significant reporting entities, which received audit disclaimers for FY 2015; data compilation and consolidation weaknesses; uncertainty with regards to the Statement of Social Insurance, the Statement of Changes in Social Insurance Amounts; and the Statement of Long-Term Projections. However, 21 of 24 of the most significant federal agencies received unqualified audit opinions. Most agency annual financial reports are audited by external, contract companies hired by agency internal auditors (Inspectors General). The GAO relies significantly on these audits as part of the audit of the CFR.

Note

1. At the agency level, financial reports are comprised of: Balance Sheet, Statement of Net Cost, Statement of Changes in Net Position; Statement of Budgetary Resources; Statement of Custodial Activity (where appropriate); Budget/cost reconciliation; Statement of Social Insurance (where appropriate); and Statement of Changes in Social Insurance (where appropriate). In addition, the 24 most significant agencies (as enumerated in the Chief Financial Officers Act of 1990) include a Schedule of Spending in the Other Information section of their annual financial reports.

Appendix 1

Glossary of terms

The definitions of terms set out below were provided to the OECD member countries as part of the survey questionnaire.

Accrual Basis: Countries are classified in this category when *i)* transactions are budgeted or recognised in the financial reports at the time at which the underlying economic event occurs, regardless of when the related cash is received or paid, and *ii)* assets and liabilities are budgeted or reported in a balance sheet, irrespective of exceptions regarding the reporting or measurement method of some specific assets and liabilities.

Cash Basis: Countries are classified in this category when transactions are budgeted or recognised in the financial reports only when the associated cash is received or paid, irrespective of their reporting of commitments.

Cash Transitioning to Accrual: Countries are classified in this category when some transactions are budgeted or recognised in the financial reports using the cash basis, and some transactions are budgeted or recognised under accrual basis. Countries that recognise all transactions on accrual basis except for tax revenue should be classified under the Accrual Basis category.

Consolidation: For the purposes of this questionnaire, consolidation means presenting the assets, liabilities, net assets/equity, revenue, expenses, and/or cash flows of public sector entities as if they were a single entity. Consolidation also implies elimination of all transactions and balances between entities that are being consolidated.

Parliamentary Appropriation: Authorisation by an act of Parliament to permit government entities to incur obligations, and/or to pay for them from the treasury. It represents the prescribed limit on spending within a specified period.

Control: The requirement for consolidation can be based on the "control" approach. Under this approach, a controlling entity should consolidate all the entities it controls, with the notion of "control" being defined in accounting standards.

Core National Government (or "Budgetary Central Government"): This comprises all central government entities that are fully covered by the central government's budget, and typically includes ministries, departments, parliament, courts of law, central government boards, and commissions. It may also include some central government agencies.

Financial Report: For the purpose of this survey, the financial report is government's key year-end accountability document. It typically comprises the financial statements and/or a budget execution statement.

OECD PUBLISHING, 2, rue André-Pascal, 75775 PARIS CEDEX 16
(42 2017 10 1 P) ISBN 978-92-64-27055-8 – 2017

www.ingramcontent.com/pod-product-compliance
Lightning Source LLC
Chambersburg PA
CBHW061220240926
51846CB00006B/1297
* 9 7 8 9 2 6 4 2 7 0 5 5 8 *